W9-CXK-786

Immunology

A SCOPE® PUBLICATION

Library of Congress Card Number 81-51715 ISBN 0-89501-009-7

Copyright 1981, 1983, 1987, 1988, 1989, The Upjohn Company, Kalamazoo, Michigan 49001
Printed in The United States of America

8801-10R6

Authors:

Ronald D. Guttmann, MD, *Guest Editor-in-Chief*
Professor of Medicine
McGill University Faculty of Medicine

Fritz H. Bach, MD
Professor, Departments of Laboratory
Medicine/Pathology and Surgery
University of Minnesota

Michael K. Bach, PhD
Hypersensitivity Disease Research Section
The Upjohn Company

Henry N. Claman, MD
Professor of Medicine and Microbiology
University of Colorado Medical Center

John R. David, MD
Professor of Medicine
Harvard Medical School

Michel Jeannet, MD
Unité d'Immunologie de Transplantation
Hôpital Cantonal, Genéve, Switzerland

Richard R. Lindquist, MD
Associate Professor of Pathology
University of Connecticut Health Center

Charles F. McKhann, MD
Professor of Surgery
Yale University School of Medicine

David Papermaster, MD
Associate Professor of Pathology
Yale University School of Medicine

Robert S. Schwartz, MD
Professor of Medicine
Tufts University School of Medicine

Contents

Preface

Today, using what is now known as "genetic engineering," it is possible to produce almost unlimited quantities of a specific monoclonal immunoglobulin after exploiting cell-fusion technology to produce a hybridoma. These antibodies can be further used to purify antigen directly, or they can be used in a "genetic engineering" procedure to clone the gene(s) for a particular antigen. After the DNA for an antigen is inserted into a microorganism such as *E coli*, almost unlimited amounts of the native antigen can be produced by the organism. In retrospect, it would have been difficult for the investigators who first studied the response to immunologic challenge to predict the production of specific antigen by these methods. Still, as in most scientific fields, these advances in molecular and cell biology progressed through a regular sequence from qualitative observation to quantitation, and then to practical application.

It is well known that the immune system is composed of both humoral antibodies and families of cells. This monograph describes compartments that are populated with T and B lymphocytes, with monocytes/macrophages, and with end-organ cells such as mast cells. Research interest is now focused on the messengers that exchange information between these various cells and that direct the final response. Besides attempting to determine the structure of these polynucleotide, polypeptide, polysaccharide, and lipid messengers, scientists must answer such fundamental questions as: What is the nature of the code used to produce and regulate the messenger? How is the code read? How is the information updated and transmitted?

The final biologic response to an immunologic challenge is fast and overwhelming, albeit controlled, and uses amplification systems that resemble those involved in blood coagulation. Of course, these amplification steps are genetically controlled, and when an error occurs at the gene level, a vital step required for the immunologic response is lost.

In the past, treatment of immunologic disorders was limited to attenuating the end-organ response with compounds such as antihistamines and corticosteroids. Today, attempts are being made to interfere with the flow of information in the immune system by the addition of trace amounts of antigens, of amino acids, and of DNA inhibitors. The end result is the same – to augment or attenuate the immunologic response.

Many immunologic problems remain; the solutions rest in the hands of those reading this monograph.

Ronald D. Guttmann, MD

Immunoglobulins

1

Antibody Structure

Antibodies are complex multichain proteins that bind antigens. All antibodies have the same overall shape, yet each has unique regions that make it fit to one antigen but not to another. As a result of this specificity, an antibody specific for wart virus will not neutralize a polyoma virus (Figure 1). Antibodies, or *immunoglobulins*, are made by plasma cells and some lymphocytes, which are widely distributed in lymph nodes, spleen, Peyer patches of the intestinal tract, tonsils, adenoids, appendix, and in the circulation. In these locations, these antibody-producing cells are ideally situated to encounter potential pathogens or foreign substances. The immunoglobulins are released into the bloodstream, lymph, colostrum, saliva, and into the lumens of the gastrointestinal, respiratory, and urinary tracts. Some antibodies remain bound to lymphocyte surfaces where they act as antigen receptors. Encounters with an antigen that reacts with the membrane-bound receptors trigger these cells to produce antibody of the same specificity.

Folding of the antibody chains creates clefts and hollows, which conform to the shape of the antigen, so that weak intermolecular forces can bind the antigen to the antibody. The region of the antibody that binds to antigen is called the *combining site*. However, closely related antigens whose molecular shapes and charge distribution are similar to the original antigen may also fit the same antibody (Figure 2a). This is termed *cross-reaction*.

Recently, it was shown that the antigen-binding site of a single antibody can react with quite different antigens. The close fit of the combining site with an antigen is created by contacts between the edges of the antigen and the amino acid side chain residues that form the walls of the combining site in the antibody. As a result, one antigen may make a sufficient number of close-range contacts to become bound; however, another antigen that contacts different residues in the same combining site may also become bound. Thus, while antibodies do show specificity and cross-reactivity with related antigens (Figure 1), each antibody may accept a very different antigen on its combining site by aligning the second antigen differently. This feature is termed *multispecificity* (Figure 2b).

Figure 1
The specificity of antibody

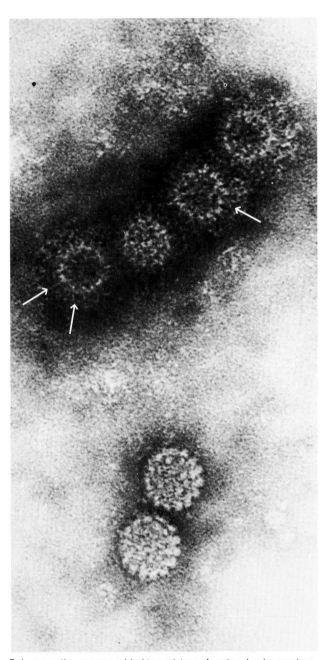

Polyoma antiserum was added to a mixture of wart and polyoma virus. Top: The smaller 450Å polyoma virus particles are coated with antibody (arrows). Bottom: The larger 550Å wart virus remains free of antibody (X 250,000).

7

Figure 2a
Two antibodies to dinitrophenol (DNP) and a cross-reaction with a related antigen

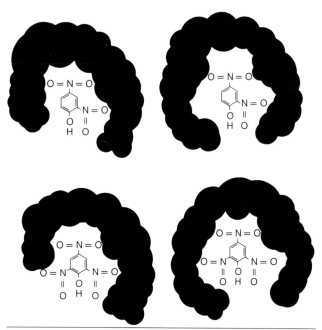

Upper left: Tightly fitting DNP-antibody combining site. Upper right: Loosely fitting DNP-antibody combining site. Lower figures illustrate cross-reactions with TNP (trinitrophenol). Lower left: Nitro groups partially block entry into tight anti-DNP. Lower right: Combining site has sufficient room to accommodate another nitro group.

Figure 2b
Multispecificity

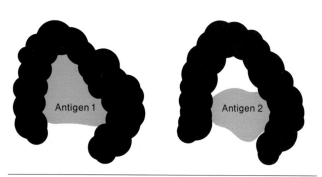

The same antibody may react with two very different antigens. This is not a cross reaction (cf 2a) but an illustration of multispecificity if the combining site has a large enough cavity and sufficient contact regions conforming to the shape of both antigens.

Usually, multispecificity is not a practical problem because the immune response is heterogeneous. The large number of different lymphocytes and plasma cells that respond to an antigenic stimulus each produce a single unique antibody. The result is the development of many different antibodies, each capable of binding to the provoking antigen.

The overall structure of all immunoglobulins is Y-shaped, with the combining sites on the end of two of the arms of the Y. The structure of these ends varies from one antibody to another. The third region, which is not involved in antigen binding, possesses other biological properties of immunoglobulins: allergic sensitization, phagocytosis, placental transfer, and complement activation. Thus, to understand the medical importance of antibodies requires an understanding of the three-dimensional shape of immunoglobulins, their subclasses, their distribution in the body, and their application in numerous modern clinical laboratory assays.

Light and heavy chains: Antibodies are formed by four polypeptide chains bonded by bridges between sulfur-containing amino acids (disulfide bonds). A pair of identical light chains (214 amino acids long) is linked to a pair of heavy chains (from 450 to 700 amino acids long) (Figure 3).

Variable and constant regions: Each antibody has a different combining site that corresponds to the structure of the antigen with which it combines. Each antibody has a unique amino acid sequence in its combining site region. There is additional heterogeneity in the antibodies made to a specific antigen. For example, not all the antibodies made against type A influenza virus have the same structure. If these antibodies are separated from all other antibodies in the blood of one person and their protein structure is determined, dozens of different antibody structures will be found, yet each will combine with influenza type A. This superimposed heterogeneity initially confused all attempts to analyze antibody structure, because a purified antibody did not have a single amino acid sequence. As a result, heterogeneity was an insurmountable obstacle until attention was turned to a curious group of proteins made by patients with multiple myeloma. These proteins, found in the blood and urine of humans and some strains of mice with multiple myeloma, resembled the antibody molecules. Also, these proteins had one unique advantage for the protein chemists – all of the myeloma protein chains from one patient were homogenous, ie, they had the same structure. This homogeneity confers a unique uniform charge to each myeloma protein so that it migrates as a single band during electrophoresis ("M" spot). If the myeloma cell produces only light chains, the chains may form a disulfide-bonded pair – the Bence-Jones protein – which is small enough to pass through the glomerulus into the urine (Figure 4).

When the amino acid sequences of the light and heavy chains of one myeloma immunoglobulin are compared with sequences of others, a striking relationship appears. All light chains have a region of highly variable amino acid sequence on the amino terminal half of the chains (Figure 3, V_L, yellow), whereas the other half, containing the terminal carboxyl group (C_L, red), is the same in all chains of the same class. Similar variability exists in the amino terminal region of the heavy chain (V_H, green), but the remaining three fourths is constant, though different from the light chain constant region (C_{H_1}-C_{H_3}, blue).

Homogeneous antibodies are occasionally synthesized in response to certain antigens, eg, streptococcal carbohydrates, and these antibodies contain a similar cluster of variable and constant regions. Newer techniques for making homogeneous antibodies in tissue culture by fusing myeloma cells and antibody-producing cells – hybridoma monoclonal antibodies – have enlarged this family of homogeneous antibodies. Conclusions derived from the study of immunoglobulins of malignant cells have been extensively confirmed by structural analysis of antibodies, so that the myeloma proteins have provided a valid simplification of the problems of antibody structure.

The genetic basis of antibody diversity: Since the number of antigens is so high, the existence of an equally large variety of antibodies is possible, each with a unique combining site. To form the combining site, polypeptide regions of the light and heavy chains are folded into their predetermined and unique shape by weak noncovalent chemical forces arising from the amino acid sequences of each chain. Thus, the amino acid sequence determines the immunoglobulin shape so that it is only necessary to vary the amino acid sequence of each combining site to create a unique antibody. Does this require an equally vast repertoire of genes in the nuclear DNA to code for each of these variable sequences? This is the genetic dilemma posed by antibody structure.

Figure 3
Schematic model of immunoglobulin molecule

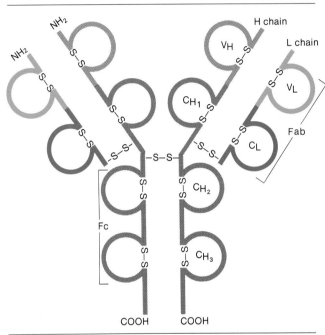

This model is composed of two heavy and two light polypeptide chains and has two antigen-binding sites (Fab) and a complement fixing site (Fc). The variable regions of the heavy (H) and light (L) chains are indicated by green and yellow loops respectively. The constant regions of the L chain are red; the multiple constant region loops of the heavy chain (CH_1 to CH_3) are blue. Folded loops of the protein chains are linked by disulfide (S-S) bonds.

The position of each amino acid in the immunoglobulin subunit chains is controlled by a sequence of three nucleotides (nucleotide triplet) in the deoxyribonucleic acid (DNA) strands of the nucleus. Faithful copying of this DNA code onto a special ribonucleic acid (messenger RNA) and the subsequent "translation" of this RNA in the cytoplasm of the cell controls the amino acid sequence of each antibody. In recent years, molecular biologists studying the genes that control immunoglobulin sequences demonstrated astonishing new relationships between the DNA in the nucleus and the amino acid sequence of the antibodies.

Theories of protein synthesis originally contained the dogma: one gene, one polypeptide chain. A rigorous application of this dogma to the amino acid sequence data of light chains would require a gene of about 636 nucleotides (ie, 212 triplets) linked together in a chromosome. Half of the gene (the part cod-

Figure 4
Two disease states with abnormal immunoglobulin fragments excreted in the urine

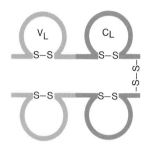

Bence-Jones protein in multiple myeloma. Two light chains are held together by a terminal disulfide bond. V = variable region, C = constant region.

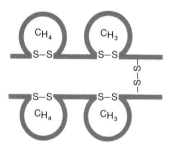

One example is "heavy chain" disease (Franklin disease), in which a portion of the heavy chain is found in the urine.

ing for the constant half of the light chain) would continuously repeat while the other half would be different in every light-chain gene. This dogma could not explain antibody diversity. Duplication of the genetic material coding for constant portions of the light chains is required, yet inheritance of genetic markers in the constant regions indicates that there is only one gene for the constant region of each class of light chains. This suggests the need for at least two gene segments to make each light chain: a V_L-gene segment that codes for the variable region of the light chain and a C_L-gene segment that codes for the constant region of the light-chain gene. Comparable V_H-gene and C_H-gene segments would code for the heavy chain.

Moving gene segments to make a protein: During differentiation of lymphocytes that make antibodies (see chapter 4), each cell is committed to make only one antibody specificity. This may occur when one of the many existing V_L-gene segments is moved, or *translocated,* to a point near the C_L-gene segment to provide a single spliced DNA region coding for messenger RNA to carry the code for the light chain into the cytoplasm from the nucleus. Similarly, one V_H-gene for the variable region of the heavy chain may translocate to a position near the C_H-gene segment to code for each heavy chain. To prove this translocation hypothesis, the sequence of the nucleotides in DNA of immuno-globulin-secreting cells was studied. The result is extraordinary. *The DNA segments that code for each of the multiple V regions are indeed separate from the DNA segments that code for the C region. They even seem to be farther apart in embryo cells than in mye-loma cells!* This raises the intriguing possibility that translocation of V-region information along the DNA is part of the process for specific commitment of differentiated lymphocytes to the synthesis of a single immunoglobulin. The segment of untranslated DNA interposed between the segments for V and C regions is copied into the messenger RNA, which is then additionally processed, and the portions that will not be translated to the amino acid sequence are excised before the protein is synthesized. Recent evidence indicates this description is oversimplified and that several more DNA segments are also involved in forming the V region. The reasons for this mechanism are unclear but may reflect more steps used in controlling commitment and differentiation of lymphoid cells. An additional DNA segment (Xp segment), coding for a short peptide region on the amino terminal end of newly synthesized immunoglobulin, lies farther away. The Xp (extra piece) peptide is only a transient component of the immunoglobulin protein chain during its synthesis on the endoplasmic reticulum of the cell and is excised during secretion to generate a new amino terminal in the mature secreted protein. This new evidence poses challenges to the older genetic concept: one gene, one polypeptide chain. Clearly, genetic information that is widely dispersed in the chromosome can be rearranged to create a new stretch of DNA, which is copied into messenger RNA. This result has enormous implications for cell differentiation in the immune apparatus and in other organs, including the nervous system.

Antibody Function

Antibody molecules have two combining sites (Figures 5a and 5b). The antibody, therefore, can act as a bivalent crosslink between two antigenic groups and bind or clump them together. This clumping – termed agglutination – helps to clear bacteria from the bloodstream. Also, clumping is the basis for many useful laboratory tests such as blood grouping.

Antibody fragments – Fab and Fc: Some protein-digesting enzymes cleave the antibody molecule into three large pieces. Two of the pieces are identical, and because they carry the antibody-combining site, they are termed the antigen-binding fragments (Fab) (Figure 3). The Fab fragment contains one entire light chain and about half of the heavy chain linked together by a disulfide bond. The third fragment lacks a combining site but has many of the other functional sites, such as those determining complement fixation, catabolism, and placental transport. This third fragment, which tends to crystallize, is called the Fc fragment (Figure 3).

Figure 5a
Rabbit anti-DNP IgG immunoglobulin saturated with a divalent DNP hapten (bis-N-DIP octamethylenediamine)

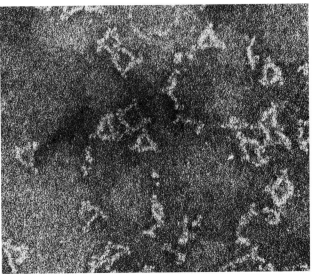

Many of the antibody molecules are linked together to form rings with regular shapes and projections from each corner (X 500,000).

Figure 5b
Antibody-hapten complex of Figure 5a after treatment with pepsin at pH 4.5 to digest the Fc fragment

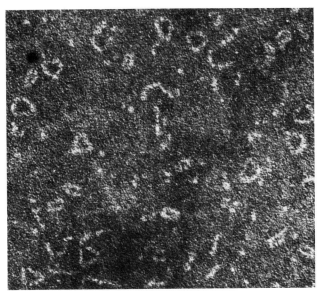

Projections at the corners of the regular shapes have been detached and appear as small pieces (X 500,000).

Immunoglobulin Classes

Beside the specific variation in each antibody molecule, which determines its specificity for an antigen, additional variation is present in the constant region of different immunoglobulin classes. These very slight changes in the Fc region govern the biological behavior of each immunoglobulin class in a general way. The variation in the constant region has been systematized into a formal classification of immunoglobulins (Table 1).

IgG(γG): The general term *immunoglobulin* has been abbreviated to Ig, so this class is called IgG. Verbally, it is often referred to as gamma G (γG). This class of antibody was previously known as γ_2-globulin, $7s\gamma_2$-globulin, and complement-fixing γ-globulin. In the human, this antibody comprises 70% of serum immunoglobulin. Its structure will be considered as a prototype for the other forms of immunoglobulin.

The IgG molecule has the usual four-chain structure of two light chains and two heavy chains. Both heavy and light chains may be used as antigens themselves and will induce the formation of antibodies to specific segments of amino acids or antigenic determinants present along the chain. In the constant regions of light chains, there are two antigenic groups: kappa (κ) and lambda (λ). Because the heavy chain has been called the gamma (γ) chain, the four chains of an IgG molecule can be diagrammatically represented as either $\gamma_2\kappa_2$ or $\gamma_2\lambda_2$. Actually, the nomenclature has become even more complex because there are now at least four antigenically different kinds of γ-chains (called subclasses) resulting from small amino acid sequence changes within the constant region of the γ-chain. The γ-chain is about 450 amino acids long; the light chain is about 212 amino acids long. The combined molecular weight of about 150,000 makes IgG one of the smallest immunoglobulins. As a result, IgG sediments fairly slowly in the ultracentrifuge and has been termed $7S\gamma$-globulin.

In the Fc region of the γ-chain is a portion of the molecule that is altered after the Fab regions have combined with antigen. This alteration activates a series of serum proteins, called the *complement system*, which assist the antibody molecule in agglutinating or lysing the antigen. The complement-activating site, or complement-fixing site, does not function until the antibody molecule has combined with antigen, causing a subtle change in shape of IgG called a conformational change. The requirement for conformational change before IgG can activate complement is necessary to protect against inadvertent activation of the complement components.

IgG subclasses, distinguished by various typing antisera, recognize small differences in the Fc regions of IgG antibodies and myeloma proteins and distinguish four γ-chain subclasses. These differences in constant regions of the γ-chain have functional significance: IgG1 and IgG3 molecules readily activate complement when bound to antigen. IgG2 antibodies are less efficient, whereas complement activation does not occur with IgG4.

Phagocytosis and cell-mediated cytotoxicity: IgG antibodies neutralize toxins and viruses in the bloodstream and tissue spaces, and they recruit phagocytic cells to help destroy larger antigens such as bacteria and cells. The IgG1 and IgG3 subclasses each have Fc regions that are avidly bound by neutrophils, monocytes, and macrophages. IgG2 and IgG4 subclasses also bind to phagocytic cells when the antibody molecules are aggregated, as they often are (eg, by complex antigens). Thus IgG antibodies, which by themselves are not directly cytotoxic, can kill cells by activating complement, binding to phagocytic cells and activating them, or inducing chemotaxis by stimulating production of complement fragments (especially C5). A small population of lymphocytes, called *killer cells*, become cytotoxic after binding to IgG molecules that are attached to target cells.

Role of IgG in the newborn: IgG crosses the placenta of an immunized mother and protects the newborn human child. No other class of antibody crosses the placenta to any significant degree. If the mother has previously been sensitized to the Rh antigen and the fetus' red blood cells carry that antigen, IgG crosses the placenta and destroys the red cells of the fetus, causing *erythroblastosis fetalis.* Paradoxically, purified anti-Rh IgG administered to mothers before sensitization by their children's cells prevents Rh sensitization. The lack of sensitization may be a result of feedback inhibition of immunoglobulin production by passively administered antibody.

IgA (γA): This class of antibody, found predominantly in saliva and secretions of the gastrointestinal tract and respiratory tract, was formerly called β2A globulin. Like IgG, it is composed of four chains – two light and two heavy. The light chains are also of the κ or λ

Table 1
Immunoglobulin Classification

Class	IgG	IgA	IgM	IgD	IgE
Spoken name (pronounced gamma)	γG	γA	γM	γD	γE
Heavy-chain name	γ (At least four gamma subclasses are known)	α (At least two alpha subclasses are known)	μ	δ	ε
Light-chain name	λ or κ in all classes		Several λ and κ subclasses are known		
Heavy-chain molecular weight	50,000	64,500	70,000	67,000	72,500
Extra chains		J chain and secretory component	J chain		
% Carbohydrate	3%	7%	12%	13%	12%
Structure	$\gamma_2\lambda_2$ $\gamma_2\kappa_2$	$\alpha_2\lambda_2$* $\alpha_2\kappa_2$	$(\mu_2\lambda_2)_5$ $(\mu_2\kappa_2)_5$	$\delta_2\lambda_2$ $\delta_2\kappa_2$	$\varepsilon_2\lambda_2$ $\varepsilon_2\kappa_2$
Functions	Fixes complement, crosses placenta, 70% of human immunoglobulins, formed in secondary response	Bodily secretions, immune response to pathogens that enter by respiratory or gastrointestinal tracts, isohemagglutinins	Early antibody, common antibody to blood group substances, fixes complement, powerful agglutinin and hemolysin	? membrane receptor on lymphocytes	Allergic responses sensitize human mast cells for anaphylaxis
Normal serum concentration (mg%)	700-1500	150-400	60-170	3.0	0.01-0.03

*IgA in serum tends to polymerize to form dimers and larger molecular-weight polymers.

type; however, the heavy chains are larger than the γ-chains of IgG and have been termed α-chains. As a result, the four-chain structure of the IgA molecule can be represented as either $α_2κ_2$ or $α_2λ_2$. Like all other immunoglobulins, the IgA molecule is made by lymphocytes and plasma cells. The cells, which are committed to production of IgA antibodies, mostly lie next to the various lumens of the body, eg, in the parotid gland, along the gastrointestinal tract in intestinal villi, beneath the bronchial mucosa, and in lactating breasts and lacrimal glands. Thus, the bulk of IgA ends up in secretions, tears, saliva, mucus, colostrum, and sweat, and only a small fraction of the total IgA produced is found in the serum. After synthesis in the plasma cells, the four-chain IgA proteins are linked together by disulfide bonds to a small peptide called the J-chain. The molecules are released into the lamina propria and transported across the epithelial cells of the mucosa into the lumen. While in transit, an additional peptide (secretory component) is attached to the IgA chains in the Fc region by additional disulfide bonds. Thus, the final form of IgA in secretion may be eight-chain IgA dimers or twelve-chain trimers. These multitrimeric forms of IgA effectively agglutinate large antigens, such as bacteria and viruses, because of their tetra- and hexa-valency.

About 7% of the weight of IgA is carbohydrate in contrast to IgG, which is only 1% to 2% carbohydrate. The role of carbohydrate in immunoglobulins is unclear.

Some people are unable to produce IgA immunoglobulin, yet they appear to be in good health. This is in marked contrast to those who have *agammaglobulinemia*, which cripples the normal immune response.

Mucosal absorption: The function of IgA is unclear, although it may protect against pathogens that invade the host through the respiratory or gastrointestinal tract. The effectiveness of oral polio vaccines may partially result from this form of immune response.

Bacterial counterattack: Of the two IgA subclasses, only IgA1 is attacked by remarkable enzymes that are produced by bacteria that are pathogenic to man because they bind to mucosal surfaces, proliferate, and colonize. *Streptococcus sanguis*, part of the *S viridans* group, is commonly found in dental plaque, the precursor of dental caries and gingivitis. *Neisseria gonococcus* and *N meningitidis* colonize the genitourinary tract and pharynx. These bacteria secrete a protease that specifically attacks the α chain to form Fab and Fc fragments. IgA2 molecules resist attack

because their α chains lack the sensitive amino-acid sequence, which is vulnerable to proteolysis. Although these bacterial proteases do not destroy the Fab combining sites, the digested IgA1 antibody Fab fragments lose their ability to agglutinate because they are no longer bivalent or, in the case of IgA1 dimers, tetravalent. Also their ability to bind to phagocytic cell surfaces is lost because the Fc region is lost. Many of these bacteria are destroyed within neutrophils after phagocytosis. This intriguing finding does not fully explain specific susceptibility to *Neisseria* species or dental caries, although these proteases may influence bacterial flora.

IgM (γM): IgM has the basic four-chain structure of two light and two heavy chains and is the largest of the immunoglobulins (molecular weight about 900,000). The heavy chain in this case is termed the μ-chain. Thus, the basic structure can be summarized $μ_2κ_2$ or $μ_2λ_2$. Five of these four-chain units are joined in a large molecule composed of 20 chains and are held together by additional disulfide bonds that join the Fc end of the μ-chain to the J-chain. The μ-chain is the largest of all the immunoglobulin heavy chains. Its molecular weight is about 70,000 in contrast to a γ-chain with a molecular weight of about 50,000. About 10% of the μ-chain's weight is carbohydrate. IgM molecules sediment rapidly in the ultracentrifuge because of their large size and have been called 19S macroglobulins. Some IgM antibodies fix complement, but most do not participate in the classic allergic reactions. On the surface of some lymphocytes, monomeric IgM molecules (with two light chains and two μ-chains) are tightly bound and may serve as antigen receptors.

Specific antibodies as antigens – idiotypes: If a myeloma protein or a homogeneous antibody is used as an antigen, several portions of the molecule may be recognized as antigenic determinants by the responding immunized host. Because of the unique sequences of amino acids in the various V_L and V_H regions, the combining site region may act as one of these determinants. Antibodies to this combining site region can differentiate this site from all others. The unique combining site determinant is called an *idiotype*, and antibodies directed against it are powerful tools in separating the steps of an immune response. IgM antibodies are the first antibodies formed after immunization. Later, the level of IgM antibody usually falls rapidly after the onset of IgG antibody synthesis. Anti-idiotype antibodies that react with the early IgM antibody-combining site regions also react with the combining sites of the later IgG antibodies. These results suggest that the differentiating clone of lymphocytes responding to an antigen first uses a pair of V_L- and V_H-gene segments coupled with C_L- and C_μ-gene segments respectively to produce specific IgM antibodies. Later, the same V_L- and V_H-gene segments are used with C_L- and C_γ-gene segments respectively to produce IgG antibodies with the same combining sites, ie, the same idiotypic determinant. Some autoimmune states in man may be a result of abnormal immune responses to self-antigens, compounded by the formation of anti-idiotypic antibodies to the anti-self antibodies.

Consequences of the large size of IgM: Because they are so large, IgM antibodies tend to stay within the vascular space and cross the capillary only with difficulty, but they do not cross the placenta in any significant amount. Thus, IgM antibodies detected in a fetal or newborn's circulation may be taken as good evidence that the baby is forming an early immune response. This is important in assessing the possibility of intra-uterine or neonatal infection. IgM antibodies are 700 to 1,000 times as efficient as IgG in agglutinating a red cell or bacterium – probably because of the many combining sites present on one IgM molecule. When a myeloma affects the cells making IgM molecules (Waldenström disease), the concentration of this large protein in the blood can rise to extraordinary levels and increase the blood viscosity so that spontaneous microthrombi and hemorrhages occur. This unusual complication can be temporarily relieved by plasmapheresis – removal of a unit of blood, separation of the cells from the plasma, and return of the cells to the patient – thus temporarily lowering the IgM level.

Relationship to ABO blood groups: Carbohydrate antigens (such as the A or B blood group substances) elicit a prolonged production of IgM antibodies rather than the usual switchover to the IgG antibody. This is fortunate because most humans normally produce antibodies to the blood groups that are not on their own red blood cells. Apparently this is caused by continued stimulation by carbohydrate groups in plants of our environment that resemble human blood group antigens. Thus the high natural level of anti-B antibody in adults with blood group A accounts for the disastrous results of a mismatched blood transfusion between the A and B blood groups. It is fortunate that these antibodies are of the IgM type, which remain within the maternal circulation. ABO incompatibility between mother and fetus is much more common than Rh incompatibility and would pose a serious threat to the fetal red cells if the natural maternal antibodies against the fetal A or B red cells could cross the placenta. Unfortunately, in rare forms of erythroblastosis fetalis, IgG antibodies to A or B antigens are formed that can cross the placenta, even if Rh compatibility exists.

IgD (γD): This class of immunoglobulin is a trace component in most sera, and its functions are uncertain. Its heavy chain is clearly distinct from the other three types already described, and it has therefore been designated the δ- chain. The structure of IgD may be summarized $\delta_2\kappa_2$ or $\delta_2\gamma_2$ with a molecular weight about the same as IgG. Like monomeric IgM, IgD is also found on some lymphocyte cell surfaces, where it may serve as an antigen receptor. Some cells may carry both IgD and IgM on their surface, each bearing the same idiotypic determinant, ie, they bear the same V_H and V_L regions on their respective heavy and light chains.

IgE (γE): This immunoglobulin has chemical properties that make it difficult to distinguish from IgA. Its heavy chain has been termed the ϵ-chain so that the structure can be summarized $\epsilon_2\kappa_2$ or $\epsilon_2\lambda_2$. IgE has a high carbohydrate content and is present in minute quantities in the serum. In normal people, only one of 10,000 immunoglobulin molecules in serum is of this class; on the other hand, allergic individuals seem to produce more antibodies of the IgE type. This immunoglobulin class governs the allergic responses of immediate hypersensitivity such as anaphylaxis and is called reagin in the allergy literature. It is also formed in large amounts in parasitic infections (see chapter 2).

The unique biological functions of IgE antibodies are localized in their Fc region. Injections of IgE antibody specific for ragweed and similar antigens into normal skin sensitize the mast cells in skin. A subsequent challenge with the allergen, even weeks later, induces the typical wheal-and-flare reaction (Prausnitz-Küstner [P-K] reaction). When the allergenic antigen combines with the Fab regions of the IgE antibody bound to its surface, the mast cell releases histamine and the slow-reacting substances of anaphylaxis (SRS-A). The histamine, in turn, dilates capillaries, alters permeability, and causes a local skin reaction. In the bronchial mucosa, the IgE antibody resides on mast cells near the smooth muscle. When the antigen combines with the Fab regions of the IgE, histamine and SRS-A are released and cause an explosive bronchial constriction characteristic of an acute asthmatic attack.

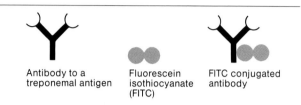

Antibody to a
treponemal antigen

Fluorescein
isothiocyanate
(FITC)

FITC conjugated
antibody

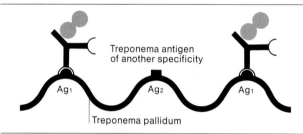

Treponema antigen
of another specificity

Ag₁   Ag₂   Ag₁

Treponema pallidum

After labeling a specific antibody with fluorescein isothiocyanate
(FITC), it can be reacted with its antigen, which can be identified
microscopically.

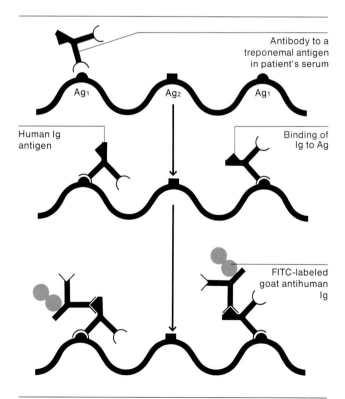

Antibody to a
treponemal antigen
in patient's serum

Ag₁   Ag₂   Ag₁

Human Ig
antigen

Binding of
Ig to Ag

FITC-labeled
goat antihuman
Ig

Serum that contains antibody is reacted with the specimen. Bound
antibody is then detected with FITC-labeled goat antihuman Ig.

Proof that the allergic function of IgE is located in its Fc region was obtained from the serum of a patient with an IgE myeloma. The IgE myeloma protein had no antibody activity. After enzymatic digestion, the IgE Fc fragment was harvested and injected into the skin of individuals allergic to ragweed, where it saturated the mast cell surface receptors usually occupied by intact IgE molecules. As a result, injected ragweed antigen could not initiate the usual wheal-and-flare reaction because the Fc region of the IgE myeloma protein on the mast cell had blocked the binding of ragweed-specific IgE to the mast cell. The antigen could combine with free IgE in the serum, but this had no ill effects. Thus, study of the molecular structure of IgE and its binding to mast cells has greatly clarified our understanding of the mechanism of allergic injury.

The IgE molecule in serum has a short half-life of only a few days. However, because the receptor site on mast cell surfaces has a high affinity for IgE Fc regions, the cell-bound IgE molecule can last for weeks on mast cells and result in prolonged hypersensitivity.

Antibodies and Antigens as Reagents

Fluorescent antibody tagging: Because of localization of the antibody-combining site in the two Fab regions, certain reagents can be coupled to other parts, such as the Fc region, without affecting the ability of the antibody to combine with antigen. For example, a fluorescent dye can be bound to the Fc region of IgG, and the resultant fluorescent antibody reagent can show where certain antigens are located in histologic sections. This method – called the direct fluorescent antibody technique – serves as a powerful tool in the rapid identification of many organisms. The syphilitic spirochete, for example, can be readily identified, thereby dispensing with the need for dark-field examination (Figure 6a). The use of fluorescent antibodies developed against carefully selected bacteria obviates delay of culture and accelerates diagnosis of such infections as Legionnaires' disease.

Modification of this technique – indirect immunofluorescence – eliminates the need for a fluorescent antibody specific for the antigen (Figure 6b). A known antigen is added to a patient's serum, then fluorescently labeled goat antibody to human immunoglobulin is added. Binding of the patient's IgG to the antigen is detected by the presence of fluorescence (Figure 7). This fluorescent reagent also detects immune complexes in the glomerulus in cases of glomerulonephritis.

Figure 7
Positive reaction of syphilitic serum to the fluorescent treponemal
antibody absorption test (indirect immunofluorescence)

Figure 7
Positive reaction of syphilitic serum to the fluorescent treponemal antibody absorption test (indirect immunofluorescence)

Protein, peptide, hormone, and drug immunoassay: In pregnancy tests, antibodies have been prepared against human chorionic gonadotropin, which appears in the urine of pregnant women. The antigen-antibody reaction provides a specific, rapid, simple, and early test for pregnancy. Peptide hormones from the human pituitary, angiotensin, and insulin may also be identified by antibodies. Some of these peptides as well as drugs and other small molecules are now measured by newer radioimmunoassay or enzyme-immunoassay methods.

Radioimmunoassay: Numerous substances in a patient's serum or other bodily fluids can be quantitatively determined by radioimmunoprecipitation. In this technique, a purified antigen (eg, a polypeptide hormone such as insulin or a protein such as IgE) is radioactively labeled. This tagged antigen is mixed with the patient's serum that contains an unknown amount of antigen. Antibodies to the antigen, such as anti-insulin or anti-IgE, are then added to the fluids, and both the radioactive and nonradioactive antigens are precipitated. The presence of antigen in the patient's serum interferes with the binding of added radioactive antigen to the antibody, because a limited amount of antibody is added. If the amount of unlabeled antigen in the patient's serum increases, more free radioactive antigen is left in the supernatant.

By determining either the radioactivity in the precipitate formed or the unprecipitated radioactivity in the supernatant, one can quantitatively determine the amount of unlabeled antigen. Calibration curves are constructed using known amounts of unlabeled antigen to allow quantitation of the concentration of unlabeled antigen in the serum (Figure 8). There are many variants of this simple, yet powerful, technique.

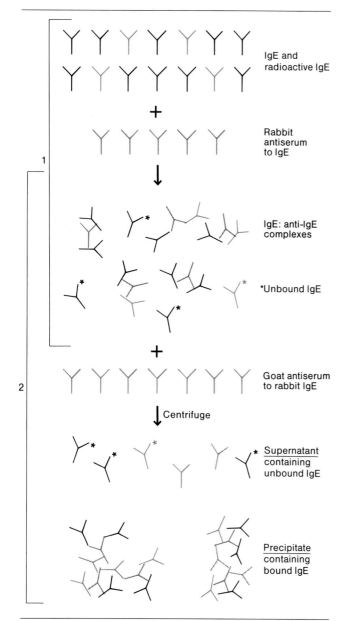

IgE and
radioactive IgE

Rabbit
antiserum
to IgE

IgE: anti-IgE
complexes

*Unbound IgE

Goat antiserum
to rabbit IgE

Centrifuge

Supernatant
containing
unbound IgE

Precipitate
containing
bound IgE

The antibody-IgE complexes formed in step 1 are precipitated by
goat antirabbit Ig antibodies (step 2). The unbound IgE* is left in the
supernatant. Either precipitate or supernatant can be counted.

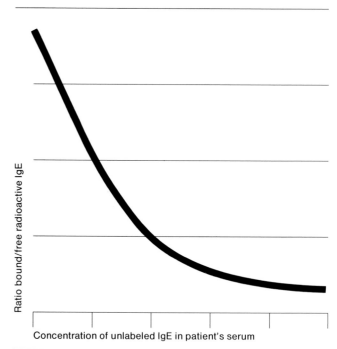

Ratio bound/free radioactive IgE

Concentration of unlabeled IgE in patient's serum

A fixed amount of radioiodine-labeled IgE competes with various
amounts of unlabeled IgE for a limited amount of anti-IgE antibodies.

Enzyme immunoassay: To avoid some of the
hazards and expense of radioactively tagged antibodies, enzymes (rather than radioactive labels) have
been coupled to antibodies. In this case, the bound anti-
body-enzyme complex is detected by its enzymatic
activity rather than by its radioactivity. If, for example,
the enzyme converts a colorless substrate to a colored
one, the appearance of the colored product after a
defined incubation interval can be measured. Small
quantities of antigen are easily detected, because one
enzyme molecule can convert thousands of molecules
of substrate into a colored product.

Immunoelectrophoresis: Antibodies to purified
components of human serum allow the rapid identification of abnormally high or low concentrations of
serum proteins. The simplest analysis utilizes immunoelectrophoresis. A serum sample in a gel is subjected
to a voltage gradient (electrophoresis), so that the
serum proteins are spread out linearly, depending on

Figure 9
Immunoelectrophoresis

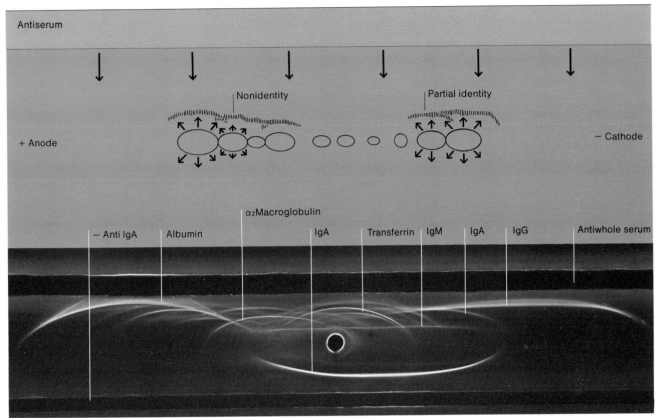

Human serum is electrophoresed in a gel and then reacted with antibody to human serum proteins. The immunoglobulins migrate toward the negative pole and albumin toward the positive pole.

Antiserum against a single immunoglobulin (i.e., IgA) can demonstrate its mobility, lower arc.

their charge. Antiserum is added to a trough cut into the gel parallel to the path of the electrophoresis. As the separated serum proteins diffuse outward, they reach the incoming wave of antibody. The antigen-antibody aggregates precipitate in a series of arcs (Figure 9). Sera of patients with disorders in the synthesis of serum proteins lack arcs in the characteristic position or show arcs in different locations. This technique readily identifies patients with abnormalities in immunoglobulin synthesis, such as agammaglobulinemia, in which case no protein arcs are visible in the region normally occupied by IgG, IgA, or IgM.

Radial diffusion immunoassay: An agar plate is impregnated with antibody, and holes in the plate are filled with a solution of antigen (Figure 10). As antigen diffuses out of the hole, it forms a ring of precipitate with the antibody already in the gel – the greater the concentration of antigen, the larger the ring diameter. By comparison with appropriate standards, one can calculate the amount of antigen in the solution that filled the hole. Radial diffusion immunoassay is now one of the simplest and most common techniques for measuring immunoglobulin concentrations in patients suspected of agammaglobulinemia.

Figure 10
Radial immunodiffusion measurement of Ig concentrations

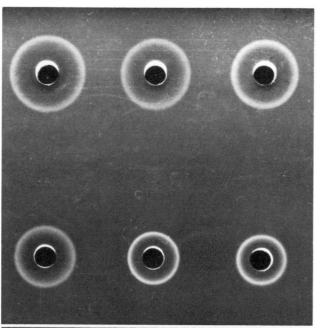

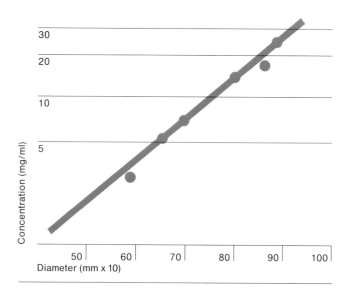

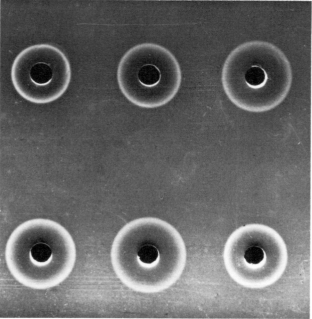

A standard preparation of human immunoglobulin G (IgG) was added at six different concentrations to wells in agar containing goat antiserum to human IgG (top panel). The diameters of the resultant circular precipitate are plotted (top right). The lower panel shows six human sera with different concentrations of IgG.

Hemagglutination: Antigens that do not precipitate readily with antibody can often be assayed after binding to the surface of a red cell, which then carries a new antigenic surface. Because of their bivalency or multivalency, antibodies specific for this bound antigen cause the red cells to agglutinate. This technique, termed hemagglutination, determines the amount of antibody in serum by measuring how much serum can be diluted before agglutination of the red cells no longer occurs. The results are then expressed as a hemagglutination titer. This technique is commonly used to quantitate antibody responses to fungi.

Conclusion
Our expanding understanding of immunoglobulin structure permits the development of new immunochemical tests, and new approaches to immunodiagnosis can be anticipated. Understanding the mechanisms whereby immunoglobulins bind to cell surfaces of lymphocytes and phagocytic cells depends on knowing how antibodies act as cellular receptors. Finally, the growing clarification of the genetic basis of antibody diversity is leading to exciting new concepts about cell differentiation.

Reagin Allergy

Introduction

The diseases and conditions involving reaginic (skin-sensitizing) allergy may be manifested in those organ systems of the body that contact the outside environment, notably the respiratory system, the skin, and the digestive tract (Table 2). The most serious disease entity in this group is asthma, with symptoms noted in the Bible. A much more common condition, hay fever, is estimated to affect 6% of the population of the United States to some degree. Hay fever was first named in 1819 by John Bostock, who described classical symptoms of seasonal allergic rhinitis in himself and in a number of his patients. The realization that etiologic agents for this condition were environmental and that sensitivity to them could be documented by an erythematous skin reaction came in 1860 with observations of Salter. By the early 1920s, Prausnitz and Küstner had demonstrated that skin reactivity to allergens could be transferred from patient to patient with serum, and Coca had given the name *reagin* to the active principle involved. It was not until 1967, however, that the Ishizakas in Denver and Bennich and Johansson in Sweden isolated human IgE and furnished convincing evidence that this newly discovered class of immunoglobulins was the most prevalent type of reaginic antibody. The discovery of IgE has led to a veritable explosion of papers dealing with its potential role in conditions that are not ordinarily classed as reagin-mediated allergy. While the dust of controversy has not yet settled, it appears that IgE antibodies may also play an important role in host defense against parasites such as schistosomes and various helminths. They may also function as "gatekeepers" in facilitating tissue inflammation and foreign-substance rejection – both primarily caused by cellular infiltrates.

Definition of Atopy or Reagin-Mediated Allergy

The term atopy, meaning strange disease, designates allergic conditions that are mediated by reaginic antibodies. The reactions are always immediate, recur chronically, and if they take place in the skin, they are associated with an edematous, wheal-type skin reaction. The tendency to atopy and the susceptibility to react to specific antigens are both inherited.

Hypersensitivity reactions have been classified by Gell and Coombs into four categories based on the nature of the antibody or effector cell, the nature of the antigen, and indirectly the time course of the reaction.

Table 2
Diseases and conditions having a presumed or proven atopic component in their etiology

Condition	Commonly associated allergens
Allergic rhinitis (seasonal and perennial)	Inhalants (spores, pollens, animal dander)
Extrinsic asthma	Inhalants (spores, pollens, animal dander)
Allergic bronchopulmonary aspergillosis	Mold spores
Atopic conjunctivitis	Inhalants (spores, pollens, animal dander)
Atopic dermatitis	Various food allergies. Drug hypersensitivities – especially to penicillins, sulfonamides, streptomycin, local anesthetics, heavy metals (mercurials and others), and reactive chemicals, eg, diazomethane
Urticarial angioedema	Insect bites, food allergies
Gastrointestinal allergy	Food allergies (cereals, milk, eggs, shellfish, fruit) and drug hypersensitivity
Chronic gastrointestinal inflammatory diseases (ulcerative colitis, regional enteritis)	Unknown
Serum sickness syndrome; anaphylaxis	Drugs, especially penicillins, heterologous antisera, vaccines, allergy extracts, iodinated radiographic material

In this classification, reagin-mediated allergy is considered as class I. Reactions involving the other types of immunoglobulins are considered as class II if the antigen is cell-bound, or class III if the antigen is soluble and tissue damage is caused by the deposition of antigen-antibody complexes. Class IV reactions are cell-mediated and are commonly considered as the reactions of delayed hypersensitivity (Table 3). However, the demarcation between humoral and cellular hypersensitivity is being progressively obliterated as we more fully understand details of both types of reactions (see also chapters 4 and 5).

Table 3
Hypersensitivity reactions

| | Type I
Anaphylactic | Type II
Cytotoxic | Type III
Toxic complex | Type IV
Cell-mediated |
|---|---|---|---|---|
| Etiology
and mechanism | Reagin (atopy) with antigen causes release of pharmacologic mediators of anaphylaxis from mast cells. | Antibody combining with tissue antigens causes activation of complement system, which causes cytolysis. | Antibody and soluble antigen form insoluble complexes that (a) deposit at various sites, causing inflammation etc and (b) cause activation of complement system. | Immune lymphoid cell reaction with antigenic cells or proteins causes (a) direct killing of antigenic cells (b) production of mediators of cell-mediated immune response causing accumulation of polymorphonuclear cells, monocytes, etc, the liberation of lysosomal enzymes, and inflammation. |
| Examples | Penicillin allergy, insect sting hypersensitivity | Systemic lupus erythematosus, poststreptococcal glomerulonephritis, rheumatic fever. | Allergic granulomatous angiitis, serum sickness, lupus nephritis, chronic glomerulonephritis. | Allograft rejection, poison ivy allergy. Breakdown may lead to chronic mucocutaneous candidiasis, failure of immune surveillance, and neoplasia. |

Symptoms, Disease Entities, Allergens

The hallmark of atopic disease is the rapid onset of symptoms, once a sensitized individual contacts the responsible allergen. As we shall see later, the response results from release of pharmacologic mediators from sensitized tissue mast cells or blood basophils (the primary site of the reaction). Therefore, the nature of the disease is in some measure determined by the route of exposure to the allergen. When the allergen is airborne (inhalant allergy), the reaction is primarily in the respiratory tract and sometimes the eyes. When the allergen is ingested (food allergy), the reaction is in the gastrointestinal tract and sometimes in the skin. When the allergen is applied to the skin, the result may be urticaria. It is important to stress that, in all cases, diseases are known that share most, or all, of the symptomatology of the atopic diseases but do not have an underlying atopic etiology. Examples are vasomotor rhinitis, food intolerance (such as the milk intolerance caused by lactase deficiency), or intrinsic asthma. In many of these conditions, the release of mediators of anaphylaxis (discussed later) plays a role in the development of symptoms. Therefore, therapy that inhibits the release or action of these mediators may still be beneficial.

In addition to the rapid-onset reaction just discussed, there is often also a second delayed reaction that begins after the acute episode has subsided, reaches a peak approximately 12 to 24 hours after initial exposure to the allergen, then gradually subsides. At one time, a concomitant delayed-type hypersensitivity to the same antigen was blamed for these symptoms. It now appears that this response can be passively transferred with purified reaginic serum and is caused by a 13-amino acid peptide that is released from mast cells.

Allergens that cause atopic responses may be either proteins with molecular weights up to many thousand or haptens such as the experimentally useful dinitrophenyl radical or the penicilloyl radical, which is derived from the metabolism of penicillin. The active allergens in various pollen extracts appear to be relatively low molecular weight peptides or proteins. They may bind to host carrier proteins before their allergenicity is expressed.

The Mechanism of IgE Production and Its Control

A number of laboratory animal models have been developed to study the production of reaginic antibodies and the reactions they initiate. Parasitic infestations, especially by helminths, are the most potent stimuli for the production of IgE antibodies (Table 4).

Table 4
Comparison of various immunoglobulins

Physical properties	IgE	IgA	IgG	IgM
Molecular weight	198,000	170,000 (monomer)	150,000	900,000
Carbohydrate (%)	10.7	7.5	2.9	11.8
Heat stability	Labile	Stable	Stable	Labile
Stability to thioalkylation	Labile	Stable	Stable	Labile
Abundance in serum (mg/ml)	0.03	2.5	10	1.2
Biological properties				
Complement activation (classic)	No	No	Yes-No	Yes
Complement activation (C_3 bypass)	Slight	Yes	Yes	Yes
Firm binding to mast cells	Yes	No	No	No
Cytophilic binding	Yes	No	Some	Some
Controls on synthesis				
Passive IgG	Inhibits	?	No effect	Inhibits
Boostable response	Only with low antigen dose	Yes	Yes	Yes; transient
Best adjuvant	Helminth, B pertussis vaccine, aluminum hydroxide gel	CFA*	CFA*	CFA*
Suppressor cells	T_S not same as IgG suppressors	–	T_S both antigen-specific and nonspecific	–
Soluble suppressor factor	Yes (mol wt 35,000 – 60,000), class-specific	–	Yes (mol wt 45,000)	–

*CFA-Freund's complete adjuvant

Under critically controlled conditions, such infestations can also enormously potentiate the reagin response to unrelated protein antigens. Other adjuvants that cause preferential production of IgE are *Bordetella pertussis* vaccine and, to a lesser extent, aluminum hydroxide gel. In general, IgE production is greatest when the immunizing regimen is only weakly stimulating. Vigorous immunization using adjuvants such as Freund's complete adjuvant usually results in a transient low-level IgE response that subsides in less than two weeks and cannot be revived by booster immunization. In this regard, IgE production differs from the production of the more abundant IgG and IgM immunoglobulins. The passive administration of homologous or heterologous IgG-containing preparations against a given antigen specifically inhibits the IgE response. The inhibition is not due to mere sequestration of the antigen by the passively administered antibody.

The synthesis of IgE is genetically determined. Evidence from inbred strains of mice, as well as from the human population, suggests a linkage between control of IgE synthesis and certain histocompatibility antigens. Animal studies indicate that regulation is a function of an immune response gene (Ia) that has been mapped between the two ends of the major histocompatibility complex (H-2 of the mouse). Besides controlling IgE synthesis, genes in the major histocompatibility complex also regulate the specific nature of the antigen that can elicit a response. These controls appear to regulate IgE and IgG synthesis in tandem (see chapters 4, 6, and 8).

Just as they do in the regulation of IgG synthesis, thymus-dependent lymphocytes (T cells) control the production of IgE by a complex series of reactions (see Table 4 and chapter 4). The initiation of IgE production is critically dependent on the presence of helper T cells. Neonatally thymectomized animals, or animals that have been treated with immunosuppressants prior to immunization, fail to produce IgE. Recent work has shown that the helper T cells involved in IgE synthesis to a given antigen are not identical to the helper T cells involved in the synthesis of IgG antibodies to the same antigen. Furthermore, the soluble helper substances involved in IgE and IgG synthesis have different molecular weights.

The role of suppressor cells is more important in the regulation of IgE synthesis than in the regulation of IgG synthesis. In fact, the transient nature of IgE synthesis in most experimental immunization protocols, especially after the use of strong adjuvants or high doses of antigen, can be explained by the induction of IgE-specific suppressor cells that restrict IgE production. Thus, if animals are thymectomized, x-irradiated (to kill thymocytes and peripheral T cells), or treated with antithymocyte serum shortly after immunization, the normally transient production of IgE becomes chronic production. However, production can be ablated by the intravenous administration of syngeneic, immune T cells.

Hyposensitization Therapy
If abrogation of an ongoing IgE response could be done safely and selectively, it would aid treatment of atopic conditions. Hyposensitization therapy, which involves the injection of extracts of allergens intradermally, presumably seeks to achieve this goal. The mechanism of hyposensitization is still unclear; neither is there agreement whether any benefits accrue. However, recent identification of the major allergen in bee venom and its use to protect bee-sting allergic individuals against a bee-sting challenge puts this therapeutic maneuver on firmer footing.

New insights into the regulation of IgE synthesis have suggested a number of experimental procedures that promise to increase the efficacy of hyposensitization. For example, some allergens are rendered less allergenic by chemical modification while retaining their immunogenic potential. Other experimental procedures are believed to convert the allergens to B-cell tolerogens that render B cells incapable of responding to the native allergen – even in the presence of helper T cells. Still other procedures appear to remove the antigenic potential of the allergens for B cells while retaining or enhancing the antigenic capacity to elicit suppressor T cells. The next few years should determine whether these approaches have practical utility in treating human volunteer recipients.

Methods for Demonstrating Atopic Conditions

The classical test for human atopy is the scratch test, or intradermal injection of antigen, a test that has been used for over 100 years (Table 5). The test reveals active cutaneous anaphylaxis and depends on the presence in the skin of sensitized mast cells that have surface-bound IgE. Upon exposure to sensitizing antigen, these cells release much of their stored pharmacologic mediators of anaphylaxis, especially histamine. The latter mediator causes localized increases in capillary permeability, expressed as a wheal-and-flare reaction (Figure 11). In man, passive cutaneous anaphylaxis can be demonstrated by injecting the presumed IgE-containing serum intradermally and later injecting the antigen into the same site. This test, which is named after Prausnitz and Küstner, requires innoculation of human sera into monkeys (Figure 12) rather than humans, to avoid the danger of transferring hepatitis to the human volunteer recipients.

The time between the injection of sensitizing serum and the injection of antigen is critical; if it is too short, there is little or no response. Maximum response requires a latent period of at least one day. Human IgE causes responsiveness in the skin for many days to many weeks, both in humans and monkeys.

Essentially the same test is routinely used in laboratory animals, except that antigen is usually injected intravenously along with a blue colloidal dye. The increased capillary permeability caused by the released histamine results in a bright blue lesion at the responding site. The increased uniformity in response achieved by intravenous administration of the antigen permits a reasonably precise quantitation of the amount of circulating antigen-specific IgE present in the serum of the donor animal (Figure 13).

A second class of reaginic antibodies has been recognized in several species of laboratory rodents. This is a subclass of IgG that is heat-stable in contrast to heat-labile IgE. The IgG subfraction is present in serum in much larger amounts than IgE, but it is not firmly bound to mast cells in the tissue. Thus, to measure this antibody, the animal must be challenged with antigen one to six hours after injection of the antibody. Antibodies of this class compete with IgE for binding sites of tissue mast cells but are eventually displaced because of

Figure 11
Typical wheal-and-flare responses to skin scratch tests for various allergens

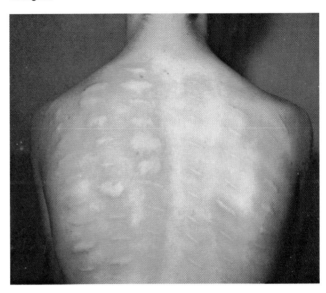

Table 5
In vivo and in vitro tests for atopy

In Vivo
Skin tests (scratch or intradermal)

Inhalation challenge

Food elimination diets with single component challenge

Prausnitz-Küstner test in monkeys

In Vitro
Histamine release from peripheral leukocytes with antigen challenge (active, passive, and serum-blocking activity)

Radioallergosorbent test (RAST) for circulating level of antigen-specific IgE

Various radioimmunologic procedures for estimation of total serum IgE

Figure 12
Prausnitz Küstner reaction to ragweed antigen E in rhesus monkey

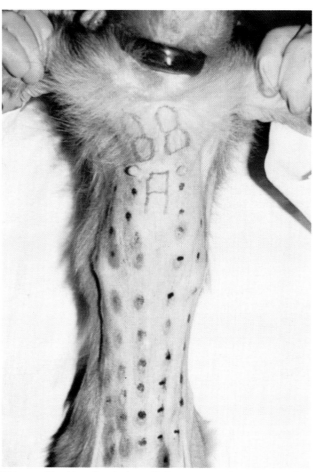

Skin sensitized two days before with human serum from a ragweed-sensitive atopic patient.

Figure 13
Passive cutaneous anaphylaxis in rats to dinitrophenol-specific rat reagin antibody

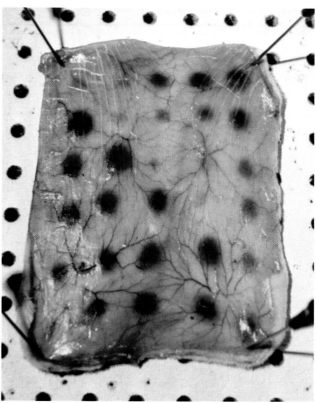

Decreasing size and intensity of the spots reflects twofold serial dilutions of the same antibody preparation.

their loose attachment. Presumably, this explains the necessary one-day lag period before full response to IgE can be elicited in the passive cutaneous anaphylaxis reaction. As yet, there is no definitive proof for the existence of a counterpart of this second class of reagins in man. However, a number of reports suggest that, under certain specialized circumstances, heat-stable reagins may also exist in man and may be important in the etiology of certain immunologic disorders. There have been several recent suggestions that asthma caused by these heat-stable IgG antibodies cannot be relieved by disodium cromoglycate (discussed later).

In vivo tests for reaginic antibody are all relatively cumbersome procedures. For this reason, various in vitro methods have been devised to study the anaphylactic reaction, the individual mediators that are elaborated, and the levels of reaginic antibodies that are present in patients' serum. Both *active* and *passive* anaphylactic reactions can be studied. In *active* anaphylaxis, cells from atopic donors are challenged with suitable dilutions of the antigen to which the donors react, and the amount of mediator that is released is quantitated. For this purpose, both histamine and the neutrophil chemotactic factor of anaphylaxis have been used. Histamine can be measured fluorimetrically, enzymatically, or by a bioassay procedure utilizing a piece of terminal ileum from a guinea pig (Figure 14). Alternatively, the cells can be equilibrated with radioactive serotonin, and the release of radioactivity following challenge can be measured on a scintillation counter. In this test, correlation between response and the clinical condition of the patient is generally good.

In the *passive anaphylactic reaction*, cells from non-atopic individuals are sensitized with serum from atopic donors; the histamine that is released upon challenge with antigen is then measured. In laboratory animals, cell suspensions are obtained by lavage of the peritoneum because these contain up to 5% mast cells.

Another related model employs tissue fragments from lungs of monkeys, guinea pigs, or from patients undergoing thoracotomy for pulmonary malignancy. In all these procedures, the production or release of all the various mediators of anaphylaxis can be assayed individually. Furthermore, the pharmacologic control of the release reaction by various drugs (discussed later) can be investigated.

In recent years, radioimmunologic methods (radioallergosorbent test, RAST) to estimate levels of circulating IgE antibodies specific for a given antigen have been developed. IgE for a serum sample is adsorbed by an allergen that is covalently bonded to a solid support. The amount of radio-iodinated heterologous antibody to IgE that becomes attached to the bound IgE reflects the amount of circulating IgE antibody (Figure 15). Although fairly good correlations have been reported, these tests suffer several drawbacks for the evaluation of the clinical state of atopic patients. First, they depend on an implied correlation between the level of circulating antigen-specific IgE and the patient's sensitivity to the antigen. This correlation is not necessarily good because only the cell-bound IgE renders the patient sensitive. The circulating antibody may be only the excess antibody remaining after saturation of the cellular receptor sites. The second drawback involves assumptions regarding the affinity of the antibody for antigen; in practice, it is likely that only very high-affinity antibodies are significant because the level of antigen at challenge is always very low. Low-affinity antibodies, if they are present and react in the assay, may imply a falsely high level of atopy. In fact, these antibodies may block mast cell receptors from attaching to high-affinity antibodies and thus help desensitize the patient from responding to challenge with low doses of antigen. Other problems with the interpretation of these tests relate to the homeostatic controls on mediator release in a given individual.

Figure 14
Schematic diagram of the procedure for bioassay of mediators of anaphylaxis having smooth-muscle contracting activity

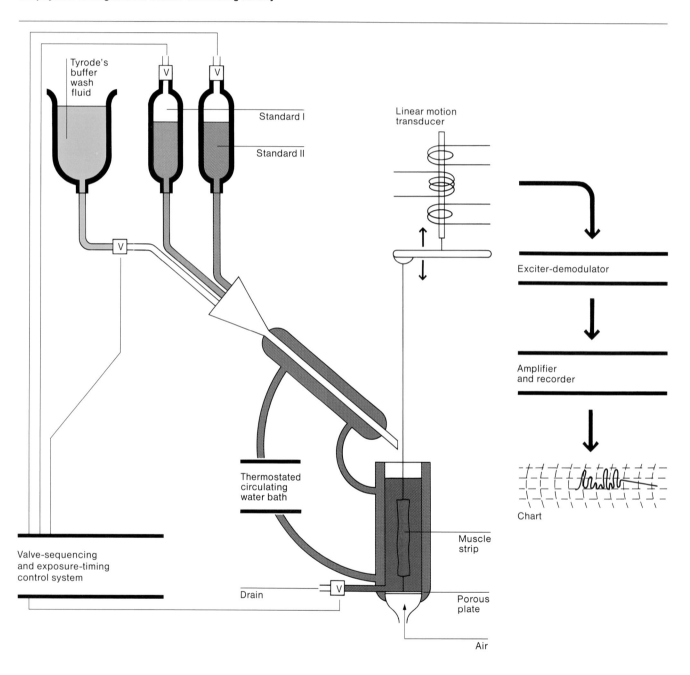

Figure 15
Schematic diagram of the radioallergosorbent test (RAST) for measuring antigen-specific IgE

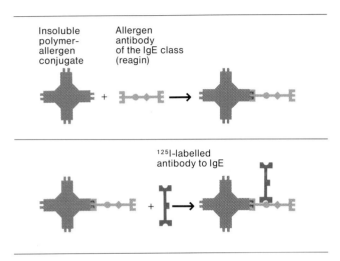

Insoluble polymer-allergen conjugate

Allergen antibody of the IgE class (reagin)

^{125}I-labelled antibody to IgE

Figure 16
Schematic representation of the changes during mediator release in mast cells (see Figure 17).

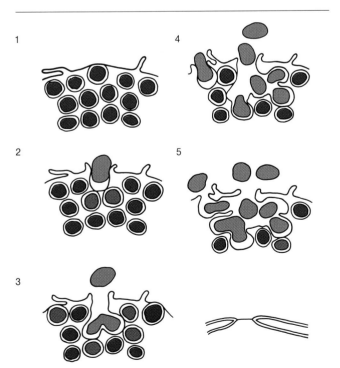

1
2
3
4
5

Pharmacologic Mediators of Anaphylaxis and Their Release

The classic mediator of anaphylaxis is histamine, a relatively low molecular weight substance of very high potency (Table 6). Histamine, along with most of the presently recognized mediators, is stored in granules in the mast cell and basophil where it is ionically bound to the anionic polymers that form the majority of the mass of the granules. During mediator release (Figures 16 to 18), the cell membrane develops invaginations that fuse with the perigranular membrane. As a result, the granule contents come into direct contact with the extracellular milieu, and the cationic mediators exchange with the much more abundant sodium potassium ions and are released into the medium. The exchange is complete in seconds or minutes and is self-limiting because the cells rarely give up all of their stored mediator. It has been demonstrated by micro-manipulative methods that the reaction is local and does not involve the entire mast cell. After the release of mediators is complete, the cell is incapable of further release, regardless of the nature of the release-initiating stimulus or the remaining store of mediators.

In addition to histamine, mast cells of some species contain serotonin (5-hydroxytryptamine). Furthermore, mast cell granules contain a host of proteins and peptides. Among these are several hydrolytic enzymes (a chymotrypsin-like protease, an arylsulfatase, an N-acetylglucosaminidase) and a series of highly specific chemotactic and cell-activating substances. The best characterized among the latter are two tetrapeptides, val-gly-ser-glu and ala-gly-ser-glu, which are collectively known as the eosinophil chemotactic factor of anaphylaxis (ECFA). Determination of chemotactic activity requires measurement of the directed migration of susceptible cells through a synthetic membrane of suitable porosity toward solutions containing the chemotactic factor (Figure 19). Accumulation of the responding cells can be determined by counting those cells that penetrate the membrane (Figure 20). All these substances are released from the mast cells along with histamine. It is clear that the chemotactic substances may play an important role in eliciting the secondary (delayed) manifestations of the atopic syndrome that were alluded to above.

29

Table 6
Mediators of anaphylaxis

	Histamine	Serotonin	Leukotrienes (LTs), slow-reacting substance of anaphylaxis (SRSA)	Eosinophil chemotactic factor of anaphylaxis (ECFA)*
Structure			 LTD	Val-gly-ser-glu Ala-gly-ser-glu
Molecular weight	97	146	500	Below 1000
Origin	Mast cell granule	Mast cell granule	De novo synthesis by mast cell, polymorph, and monocytes?	Mast cell granules
Biosynthesis	Histidine decarboxylation	Tryptophan decarboxylation	From arachidonic acid via oxidation with 5-lipoxygenase, reaction with glutathione, and loss of glutamic acid	Unknown
Action	Vasodilator	Vasodilator	Slow-acting vasodilator	Chemotactic primarily for eosinophils
Assay	Fluorimetric, enzymatic, or in muscle bath with atropinized guinea pig ileum	Fluorimetric	Muscle bath with atropinized, antihistamine-blocked guinea pig ileum	Boyden chamber with eosinophil-rich leukocyte preparation

*Other chemotactic proteins and peptides with specificities
for various leukocytes have also been recognized.

Figure 17
Events that accompany mediator release

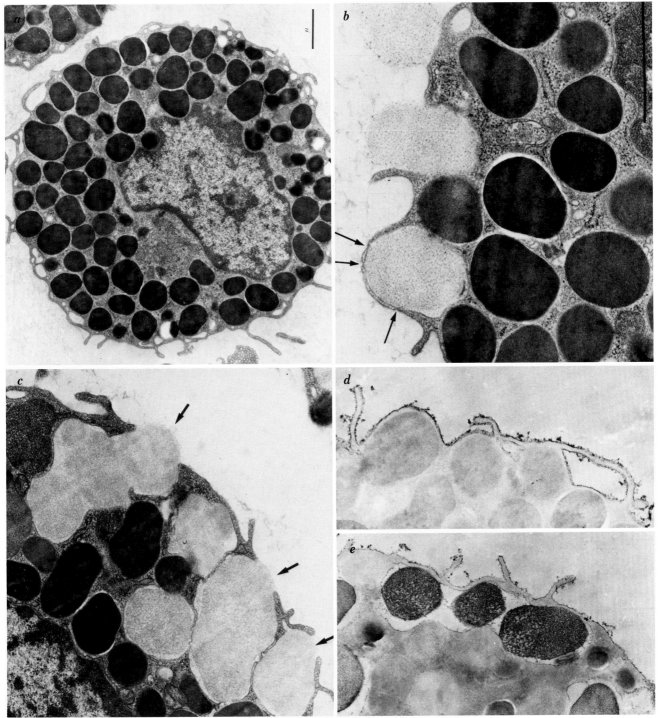

(a) Normal mast cell. (b) Mast cell 20 seconds after initiation of release. (c) Mast cell 40 seconds after initiation of release. Note developing invaginations and decreased electron opacity of adjacent granules. (d,e) Normal mast cell membrane and challenged mast cell membrane reacted with lanthanum chloride, an extracellular electron stain. Note accumulation of dark staining lanthanum granules in perigranular vesicles in challenged mast cell in e.

Figure 18
Comparison of normal and degranulated rat mast cells

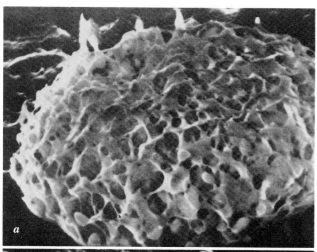

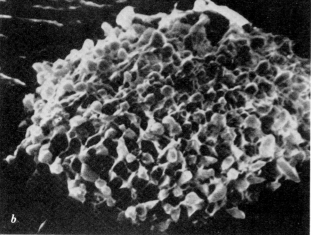

(a) Appearance of a normal rat mast cell in the scanning electron microscope. (b) Appearance of a degranulated rat mast cell in the scanning electron microscope.

Figure 19
Schematic diagram of the procedure for determination of chemotactic activity

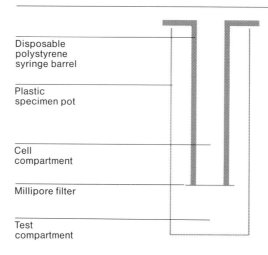

Disposable
polystyrene
syringe barrel

Plastic
specimen pot

Cell
compartment

Millipore filter

Test
compartment

Figure 20
**Infiltration of eosinophils into site of passive cutaneous
anaphylactic reaction**

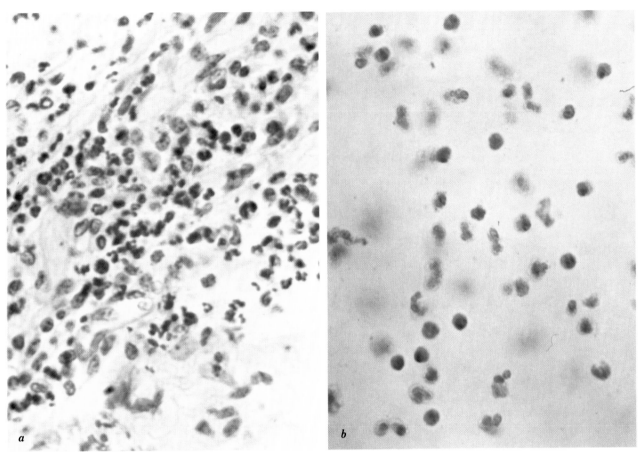

(a) Tissue infiltration by eosinophils at the site of a passive cutaneous
anaphylactic lesion in guinea pig skin. (b) Appearance of a positive
ECFA assay. For quantitation the number of eosinophils per unit of
membrane area is enumerated.

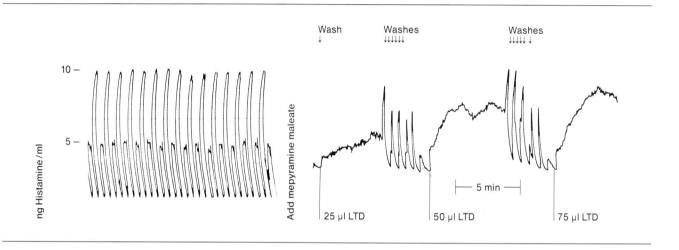

Figure 21
Typical assay result for histamine and leukotrienes using a muscle strip of the terminal ileum of the guinea pig

In contrast to histamine, serotonin, and the chemotactic substances, slow-reacting substances of anaphylaxis (SRS-A) are not present in the cells in preformed state but are synthesized by mononuclear cells after the primary activation of the tissue mast cells. In addition, the rate of release of SRS-A differs from the rate of release of the other mediators from the mast cell granules. SRS-A belongs to a series of compounds called the leukotrienes, which are metabolites of arachidonic acid that have three conjugated double bonds and a hydroxyl group. In addition, the leukotrienes C, D, and E have a thioether linkage to cysteine (LTE) that may be linked in turn by a peptide bond to glycine (LTD) or to glycine and glutamic acid (LTC). The assay for histamine (Figure 21) can also be used to determine LTC, D, and E, provided antihistamines are added to the bath. On a weight basis, LTD is 100 to 1,000 times more potent than histamine but the contractions are characteristically slower and more difficult to "wash out" (Figure 21). To improve the differential identification of LTD, a specific inhibitor, FPL 55712, may be added to the bath.

Human bronchial muscle is uniquely sensitive to LTD, which may explain why patients with asthma derive little benefit from antihistamines. Thus, LTD may be a major etiologic agent in human asthma. It is the only known mediator specifically produced during anaphylaxis that is not antagonized by antihistaminic compounds but causes smooth muscle contraction. Only now are the many pharmacologic activities of the leukotrienes being described.

Pharmacologic Regulation of Mediator Release and Mediator Action

The usual treatment of atopy utilizes corticosteroids, catecholamines, and inhibitors of cyclic adenosine monophosphate phosphodiesterase (eg, theophylline). The smooth muscles that line the airways are controlled by the sympathetic and parasympathetic nervous system, as are all other smooth muscles. In the lungs, the parasympathetic system is the primary constrictor system, whereas sympathetic nerve stimulation results in relaxation. The sympathetic receptors of this tissue are predominantly of the β-type that respond to epinephrine and isoproterenol and are blocked by propranolol. Using selective β-adrenergic stimulators, it was found that bronchial muscle has a β_2-type response in contrast to the β_1 response of cardiac muscle. Therefore, β_2-selective sympathomimetic drugs, such as salbutamol and terbutaline, are receiving increasing interest in the management of asthma.

The same receptor specificity for neurohormones also governs modulation of the release of anaphylactic mediators by mast cells. The role of the adenylate cyclase system and cyclic adenosine monophosphate in the catecholamine-dependent regulatory system has been documented in mast cells in humans and monkeys. Also, prostaglandins may affect this system when used in very low concentrations, depending on the organ and species from which the mast cells are obtained. Although a transient rise in cellular cyclic AMP concentration is essential for mediator release (Figure 22), prolonged increases result in inhibition of release, probably because of uncoupling of key kinetic events in the release reaction.

In addition to the combination of IgE and allergen, a variety of experimental manipulations can elicit mediator release from mast cells. While some of these manipulations are strictly artifactual, others may have some bearing on the situation. Similarly, a variety of nonimmunologic stimuli can stimulate mediator release, so its inhibition may be beneficial, regardless of the underlying cause for mediator production.

Mediator release is a model of secretory function in general and has been the subject of many studies seeking the sequence of biochemical events that ultimately leads to the release of mediator. These studies have shown that, regardless of the signal used to induce mediator release, the terminal sequence of events seems to be the same. The active uptake of extracellular calcium by the cells is the final common signal that leads to release (Figure 22). In fact, a calcium ion-specific ionophore can by-pass all the pharmacologic controls on the mediator release reaction in experimental systems by rendering the cells selectively permeable to calcium.

Table 7
Suggested management of atopic conditions

Removal of allergen	Specific foods, animal dander, dust, pollen.
Hyposensitization therapy	Chronic injections of allergen-containing extracts. Mode of action unknown.
Disodium cromoglycate	Chronic, prophylactic, by insufflation. Prevents mediator release.
Corticosteroids, ACTH	Various acute regimens to alleviate symptomatology (orally, topically, or by injection).
Catecholamines	Isoproterenol, epinephrine, etc. Acutely to neutralize an attack. (By inhalation, orally, or by injection.)
Methylated xanthines	Theophylline, aminophylline, etc, inhibitors of cyclic adenosine monophosphate phosphodiesterase, synergize the effect of catecholamines causing increased intracellular concentrations of cyclic adenosine monophosphate, decreased mediator release, and decreased smooth muscle contraction. (By suppository or oral administration.)
Antihistamines	Block the effects of histamine.

A new mode of treatment for atopic conditions, and especially for asthma, has recently received considerable attention. Such therapy is based on the observation that a number of cromone acids prevent release of mediators during any of the physiologic or immunologic histamine-release evoking reactions. One of these substances, disodium cromoglycate (cromolyn sodium), is now clinically used. The exact mechanism of action of the cromone acids is unknown, but they apparently bind to the target tissue for a very short time. Nevertheless, if a release reaction is initiated while the drug is bound, no release occurs and the cells resist subsequent attempts to elicit mediator release (Table 7, Figures 22, 23). These inhibitors can inhibit mediator release even when the release is initiated by the calcium ionophore. This suggests that the cromone acids may act by blocking the calcium channels in the plasma membrane, which must open following cell activation. However, it is now clear that the efficacy of cromolyn sodium may not be related to its ability to block mediator release but rather to other, still poorly understood, indirect effects.

With the increased understanding of reagin allergy have come new approaches to the rational treatment of these conditions. Hopefully, some of these approaches will lead to new therapies in the future.

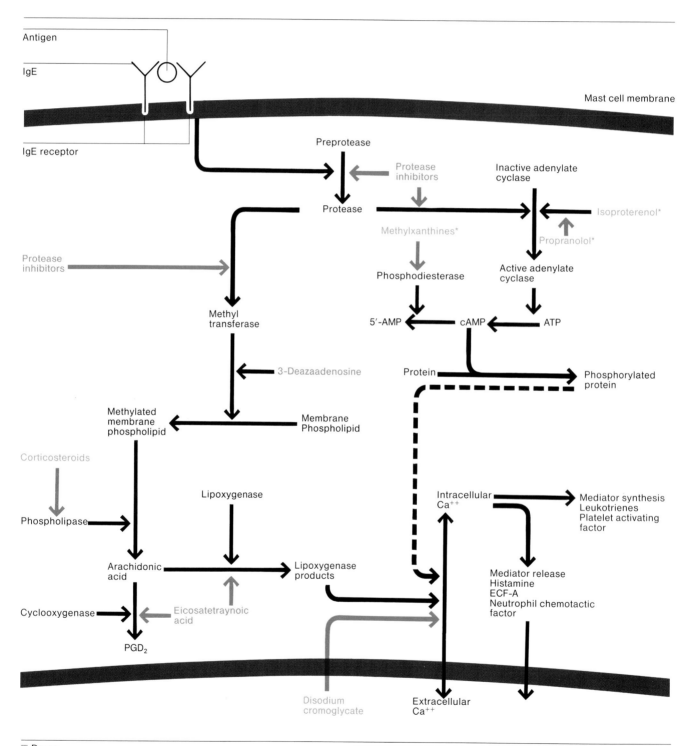

Antigen

IgE

Mast cell membrane

IgE receptor

Preprotease

Protease inhibitors

Inactive adenylate cyclase

Protease

Isoproterenol*

Methylxanthines*

Propranolol*

Protease inhibitors

Phosphodiesterase

Active adenylate cyclase

Methyl transferase

5′-AMP   cAMP   ATP

3-Deazaadenosine

Protein   Phosphorylated protein

Methylated membrane phospholipid

Membrane Phospholipid

Corticosteroids

Lipoxygenase

Intracellular Ca⁺⁺

Mediator synthesis
Leukotrienes
Platelet activating factor

Phospholipase

Arachidonic acid

Lipoxygenase products

Mediator release
Histamine
ECF-A
Neutrophil chemotactic factor

Cyclooxygenase

Eicosatetraynoic acid

PGD₂

Disodium cromoglycate

Extracellular Ca⁺⁺

▓ Drugs
▓ Pharmacologic agents

*Persistent activation of adenylate cyclase inhibits release; transient activation is essential for release.

Figure 23
Structural formulas of commonly used drugs

Disodium cromoglycate

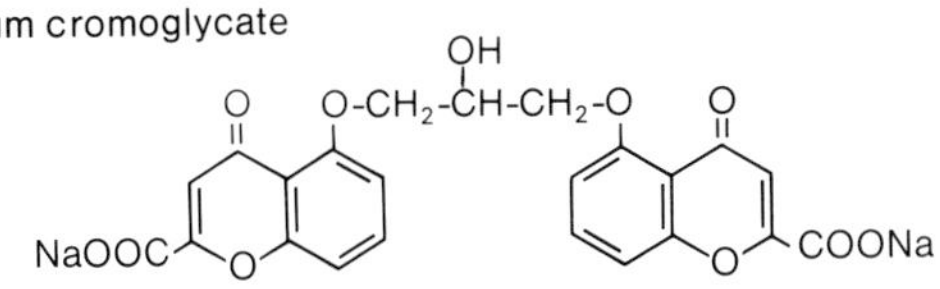

Epinephrine

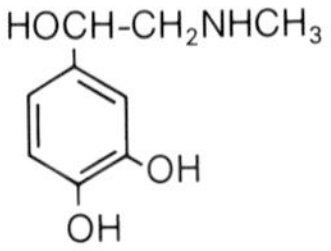

Isoproterenol

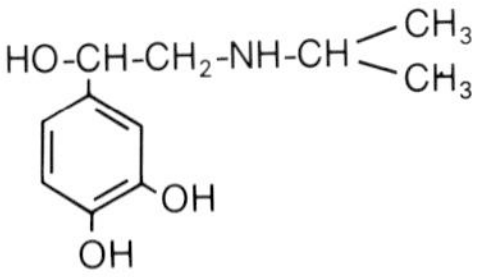

Salbutamol

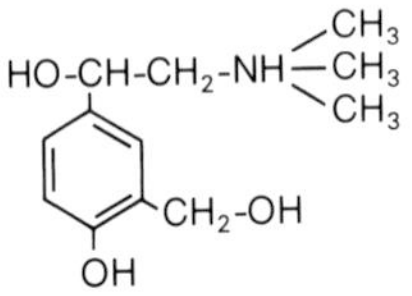

Theophylline

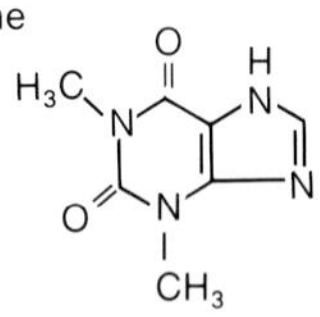

Hydrocortisone

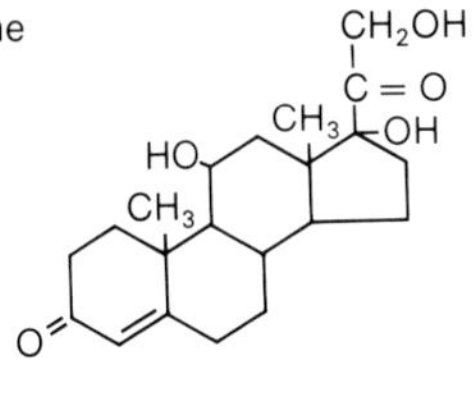

Immediate Hypersensitivity

3

Introduction

The immune system normally protects the organism against foreign substances, but occasionally the system attacks the cells of the organism and destroys them. Both the beneficial and the deleterious reactions are divided into two types: immediate and delayed. Immediate reactions are visible within minutes or a few hours. They are initiated by humoral antibodies, the products of B lymphocytes. Delayed reactions require many hours, even up to several days, to become manifest. Such reactions are mostly initiated by T lymphocytes and do not involve humoral antibody. This chapter concerns those immediate-type reactions that have a deleterious effect on the host. They are commonly referred to as immediate hypersensitivity reactions.

Soon after the protective action of the immune system was discovered, Portier and Richet found, while attempting to develop immunity in dogs against toxins from the sea anemone, that the second injection of a nontoxic amount of the sea anemone toxin made the dogs violently ill, and frequently they abruptly died. This apparent increased susceptibility to the toxin was called *anaphylaxis*. Not long after, Arthus found that intradermal injections of antigen into previously immunized animals produced local inflammation and necrosis at the site of antigen injection. This local reaction is called the *Arthus reaction*, whereas the generalized systemic reaction is called *serum sickness*.

The interaction of antibody with its corresponding antigen is rarely harmful to the host. Usually some additional amplifying or mediator mechanism is needed to harm the host. There are several effector systems, and they serve as a convenient way of classifying immediate-type hypersensitivity reactions (Figure 24). A common denominator of these diverse effector mechanisms is the requirement for the crystallizable fragment (Fc) of the antibody molecule. Following antibody-antigen interaction, the Fc portion activates the nonspecific biological effector mechanisms that actually injure the host (see chapter 1).

Figure 24
Immediate-type hypersensitivity reactions

Reactions requiring antibody

Reactions requiring antibody and complement

Reactions requiring antibody and macrophages

Reactions requiring antibody and mast cells

Reactions requiring antibody, complement, and mast cells

Reactions requiring antibody, complement, and polymorphonuclear leukocytes

Reactions requiring immune complexes

Reactions Requiring Only Antibody

Immediate hypersensitivity reactions that follow the combination of antibody and antigen, but without amplifying effector mechanisms, are rare. However, examples do exist: some patients with diabetes mellitus develop resistance to insulin-replacement therapy because they develop antibodies to insulin and inactivate the insulin. In acquired hemophilia, antibodies develop to one of the coagulation factors, most commonly factor VIII, and neutralize its potential enzymatic function in the coagulation sequence. In these instances, antibodies specific to insulin or clotting factor VIII inactivate the respective antigens' function by covering or sterically hindering the active site or by altering the tertiary structure of the molecule. The resultant hypersensitivity is strictly a result of depletion of the active insulin or the clotting factor.

38

Reactions Requiring Antibody and Complement

While studying the lytic properties of antisera, it was discovered that both specific antibody and nonspecific factors found in fresh serum were required for cell lysis. These factors, which work with many antibodies, are called the complement system (C).

The classical complement system consists of nine separate components (numbered C1 through C9) that, when activated, interact sequentially with one another in a "water fall" or "cascade" fashion, which resembles the coagulation sequence. The individual components are numbered in the order of their discovery, so the numbering does not follow their order of activation. Only C4, however, is out of sequence; so the order of activation is C1, C4, C2, C3, C5, C6, C7, C8, C9.

Activation of some of the components of the complement system results in the cleavage of a component into two fragments. In some cases, the larger of the two fragments joins the preceding activated component to generate a new enzymatic activity that can cleave the next component. Frequently, the smaller fragments generated in the early steps possess important inflammatory properties such as neutrophil-attracting (chemotactic) activity of C3a and C5a.

Activation of the complement sequence during immune cytolysis is illustrated in Figure 25. The first component of the complement system consists of three separate proteins, C1q, C1r, and C1s, held together as a trimolecular complex by the calcium ion. Binding the C1q subunit to at least two adjacent Fc portions of immunoglobulin molecules activates C1q. A single molecule of IgM or at least two IgG1, IgG2, or IgG3 molecules close to each other provide the Fc portions. IgG4, IgA, and IgE cannot activate C1. By an autocatalytic reaction, C1r is activated, and this, in turn, activates C1s. Activated C1s, or $\overline{\text{C1s}}$, (bars above the numbers are used to indicate activated complement components exhibiting enzymatic activity) have both esterolytic and proteolytic activity; $\overline{\text{C1s}}$ splits its two natural substrates C4 and C2 into two fragments. The larger C2 fragment is a proteolytic enzyme; the smaller C2 fragment possesses kinin-like activity (discussed later). The larger fragments of activated C4 and C2 join together to form a bimolecular complex C42, also called C3 convertase, that cleaves C3. This is an important amplification step because one bimolecule of $\overline{\text{C42}}$ produces several hundred activated C3 molecules.

Figure 25
Schema of complement cascade

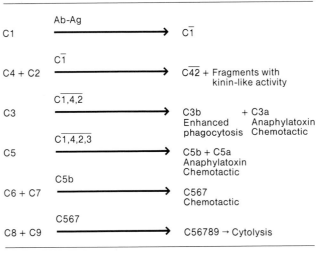

The enzymatic splitting of C3 also produces a low molecular weight fragment (C3a), called anaphylatoxin, which can induce histamine release, mimicking the symptoms of anaphylaxis. The larger C3 fragment (C3b) combines with $\overline{\text{C42}}$ to form C5 convertase, ($\overline{\text{C423}}$), which splits C5 into C5a (another anaphylatoxin) and C5b. C5b, in turn, binds stoichiometrically with C6 and C7 to form a trimolecular complex (C567, which binds to the cell membrane and serves as the focal point for the further binding and detergent-like lytic action of C8 and, especially, C9. C567 may be bound to the cells with membrane-associated antibody and early complement components, or it may exist in the fluid phase, where it can react with unsensitized cells (innocent bystander reaction). C567 is also chemotactic for polymorphonuclear leukocytes (PMNs) and so participates in the inflammatory process.

Figure 26
Binding of a complement component to the surface of a red blood cell

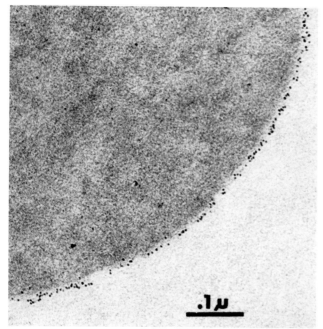

The small black dots on the surface of the red blood cell are ferritin molecules, which are attached to an antibody that is reacting with C3 bound to the erythrocyte membrane. This particular erythrocyte has about 450 C142 molecules and over 100,000 C3 molecules (X 95,000).

Figure 27
Electron micrograph of a negatively stained human erythrocyte membrane

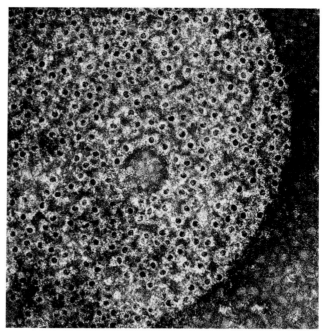

C5 produces these apparent holes in the membrane. These holes are not functionally significant, however, as the cell retains its normal permeability. Functional holes develop after C8 and C9 bind to the erythrocyte membrane and intracellular ions and hemoglobulin leak out (X 400,000).

Once C567 binds to the membrane, C8 joins the tri-molecular complex, and up to six binding sites for C9 develop on C8. The resulting decamolecular complex alters the cell membrane so that water and ions can enter and rupture the cell. In fact, binding of C5 to the cell's membrane doubles the membrane's thickness and produces structural alterations that resemble holes 100A (10 nm) in diameter. However, the cells do not leak. Only after the assembly of C8 and C9 (Figures 26 and 27) do functional holes appear.

The complement cascade is regulated by both intrinsic and extrinsic mechanisms. Intrinsic regulation is afforded by the natural instability and short active life of some of the complement components. Extrinsic factors include serum inhibitors, such as C1 inhibitor, C3b inactivator, C6 inactivator, and ana-phylatoxin inactivator, which inhibit the biological activity of specific factors of the complement cascade.

Alternative Pathway of Complement Activation

There are two pathways for activation of complement: the classical pathway and the alternative pathway. The classical pathway requires factors C1 through C9. The alternative pathway, previously referred to as the properdin system or the alternate complement pathway, also uses factors C6 through C9 as the terminal portion of the pathway. Figure 28 diagrammatically shows the early steps of the alternative pathway. The physiochemical characteristics of the proteins and their mechanism of interaction parallel those in the early classical pathway. The resultant C3- and C5-cleaving enzyme is distinct from, but analogous to, $\overline{C42}$ and $\overline{C423}$. In effect, the alternative pathway bypasses C1, C4, and C2 of the classical pathway.

Activation of the alternative pathway is initiated by aggregated immunoglobulins IgG1 to IgG4, IgA, and IgE. Unlike the classical pathway, the initiation site is in the Fab domain of the immunoglobulin molecule. In addition to activation by immunoglobulins, the alternative pathway is triggered by bacterial endotoxins, yeast cell walls (zymosan), high molecular-weight polysaccharides such as inulin and agar, cobra venom factor (snake C3b), and nephritic factor, a pathologically synthesized autologous protein that possesses the structure of an antibody and initiates and stabilizes the formation of C3bBb.

Both intrinsic and extrinsic mechanisms regulate the activity of the alternative pathway. Intrinsic mechanisms are comparable to those present in the classical pathway, ie, innate instability and short active life of some of the activated components. Two proteins, beta-1H globulin and C3b inactivator, provide extrinsic regulation of the active C3 fragment (C3b), the C3-containing C3 and C5 cleaving enzyme (C3bBb), and the stabilized enzymes of properdin (PC3bBb) and of initiating factor (IFC3bBb).

Complement and Inflammation

To this point, we have limited our consideration to the cytolytic effects of complement activation, but, in addition, the complement system plays a very important role in the inflammatory process. As already mentioned, activation of C2, C3, and C5 yields two proteins: the large fragment is responsible for sequential activation of the sequence and ultimate cytolysis; the smaller fragment initiates and participates in the inflammatory process. The active molecules produced by C3 and C5 activation are C3a and C5a and are called anaphylatoxins. The anaphylatoxins have relatively low molecular weights (approximately 8,000 to 15,000 daltons) and can cause smooth muscle to contract and increase vascular permeability by releasing histamine from mast cells.

In addition, C3a and C5a are chemotactic and attract polymorphonuclear leukocytes to the site of their production. Normal serum contains natural inhibitors of chemotactically active molecules that regulate the extent and the magnitude of polymorphonuclear leukocyte influx into an inflammatory site. Cleavage of C2 liberates a kinin-like moiety that contracts smooth muscle and increases vascular permeability through a mechanism that does not involve histamine release. C567 also attracts polymorphonuclear leukocytes. Thus, activation of the complement sequence elaborates factors that both initiate and amplify the inflammatory process.

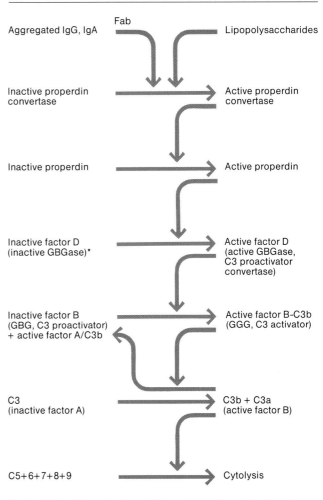

Figure 28
Schema of alternative pathway of complement activation

*Alternate terminology

Although we are concerned with the mechanisms of antibody-induced injury, an important factor is the participation of the complement system in inflammation that is not induced by antibody. For instance, lysosomal enzymes released following tissue injury cleave some inactive native complement components into active fragments with phlogistic properties. Polymorphonuclear leukocytes that accumulate within areas of myocardial infarction are, in fact, attracted by the chemotactic activity of C3a that is cleaved from C3 by lysosomal enzymes released from dying myocardial muscle cells (Figure 29).

Figure 29
The inflammatory sequelae of complement activation

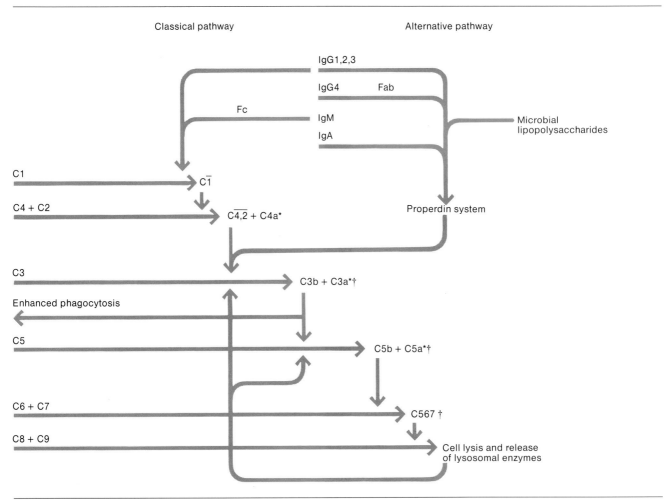

Classical pathway   Alternative pathway

*Increased vascular permeability and
 smooth muscle contraction
†Leukocyte chemotaxis

In addition to complement, other enzyme effector systems in plasma interact to initiate and amplify inflammatory reactions. These systems include the clotting system, the plasmin (fibrinolytic) system, and the kinin system. Although these complex interactions are under continued investigation, the initial observation that immune complexes added to blood or plasma activate the clotting system has been known for some time. In part, this is caused by the clumping and adherence of platelets to C3b in the immune complex (immune adherence) and the secondary release of clot-promoting platelet factor 3. In rabbits, activation of C6 appears to promote clotting by an incompletely understood mechanism. In humans, C6 is also implicated in the clotting process.

Hageman factor (clotting factor XII) plays a pivotal role in the clotting, kinin, and fibrinolytic systems (Figure 30). Activation of Hageman factor initiates the intrinsic coagulation sequence and activates the plasmin system. Plasmin, in addition to cleaving polymerized fibrin into vasoactive fibrinopeptides, cleaves activated Hageman factor into Hageman factor fragments. The latter, in turn, activate the kinin system. The net result of kinin system activation is increased vascular permeability, chemotaxis of polymorphonuclear leukocytes, pain, and production of fragment Kf, which enhances the functional efficiency of the production of $\overline{C42}$. Plasmin also initiates the complement cascade by enzymatically activating the C1s subunit of C1. Additionally, plasmin directly generates anaphylatoxin (C3a) from C3. To regulate these interlocking events, C1 esterase-inhibitor, in addition to controlling the complement system, inhibits plasmin, kinin generation, thrombin, and activated Hageman factor. Thus, through a very complex series of molecular interactions, the clotting, clot lysis, kinin, and complement systems amplify one another to elicit the inflammatory response. The presence of multifunctional protease inhibitors in serum regulate many enzyme components in these four effector systems and thereby regulate the intensity of inflammation.

Reactions Requiring Antibody and Macrophages

Not all antibody-antigen reactions cause complement fixation. In fact, most immune hemolytic anemias do not trigger the complement cascade. The antibodies involved in most such immune hemolytic anemias are of the IgG class, and when bound to the erythrocytic membrane, they are too widely separated from one another to activate C1. Although complement is not fixed, the erythrocytes are nonetheless destroyed by macrophages of the reticuloendothelial system. Macrophage cell membranes possess receptors for the Fc portion of certain classes of immunoglobulins called cytophilic antibodies. Cytophilic antibody should not be confused with cytotropic IgE antibodies (discussed later), which bind to mast cells and basophils. The exact mechanism by which the macrophage destroys the erythrocyte in the presence of cytophilic antibodies is not known. Somehow, erythrocytes are held in intimate contact with macrophages by the antibody and are destroyed. However, phagocytosis is not necessary for the destruction of erythrocytes by macrophages.

Recent evidence indicates that lymphocytes can also serve as effector cells in antibody-induced cell injury. Lymphocytes, which are neither T cells nor B cells (see chapter 4), are the most likely effector cells, and they seem to work by a mechanism similar to that used by the cytolytic T lymphocytes. Most of the experimental work on antibody-dependent cell destruction that is mediated by lymphocytes has been in the field of transplantation immunity.

Reactions Requiring Antibody and Mast Cells

Mast cells are reservoirs for histamine and serotonin, and their release is an important effector mechanism in immediate hypersensitivity. These vasoactive amines increase vascular permeability and promote edema formation by opening gaps between endothelial cells of postcapillary venules. They also contract smooth muscle and stimulate exocrine gland secretion.

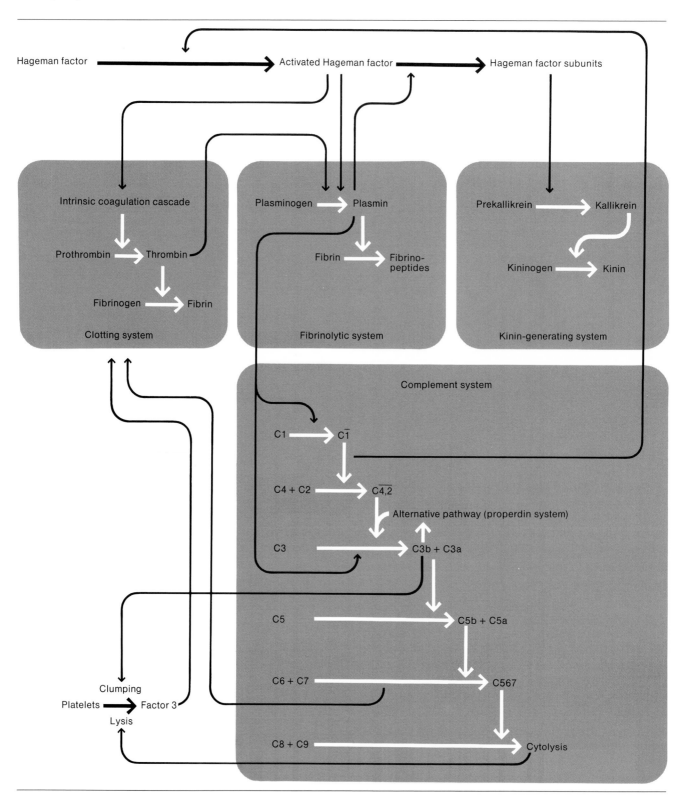

Several mechanisms exist for the release of vasoactive amines from these reservoirs. The most important of these involves antibodies of the IgE immunoglobulin class. These IgE molecules are cytotropic; they attach to receptors on mast cells and basophils by the Fc portion of the immunoglobulin molecule. When specific antigen combines with two adjacent antibody molecules bound to the surface of a mast cell, the mast cell actively releases the vasoactive amine stored in its cytoplasmic granules. If this reaction occurs in the lung, as it does in some species (including humans) during systemic anaphylaxis, there is bronchiolar constriction, edema formation, and increased mucous secretion (Figure 31).

Reactions Requiring Antibody, Complement, and Mast Cells

Anaphylaxis is divided into two types: the cytotropic IgE-dependent type described in the preceding section and a type requiring both immunoglobulin complexes and complement. As already discussed, during the activation of C3 and C5, two different low molecular-weight anaphylatoxins are produced (C3a and C5a). These anaphylatoxins independently provoke mast cells into releasing their vasoactive amines by reacting with distinct receptors on the mast cell's surface.

In some species, platelets are reservoirs of vasoactive amines that are released by platelet lysis or clumping about immune complexes. Activation of terminal complement components by nonparticulate immune complexes can lead to complement-mediated lysis of closely associated "innocent bystander" platelets. Particulate immune complexes in the presence of C3b promote immune adherence of the platelets to the complexes. The result is loss of vasoactive amines without platelet lysis. Thus, a second, and probably less important, mechanism leads to systemic anaphylaxis.

Figure 31
The IgE-mediated release and action of vasoactive amines

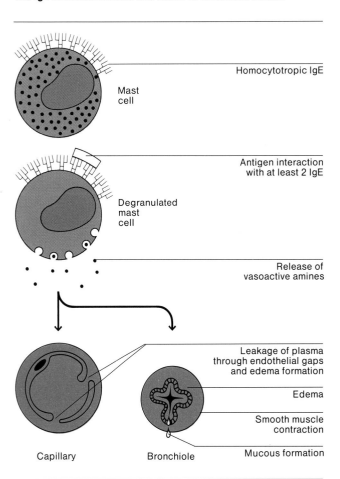

Mast cell — Homocytotropic IgE

Degranulated mast cell — Antigen interaction with at least 2 IgE

Release of vasoactive amines

Capillary — Bronchiole

Leakage of plasma through endothelial gaps and edema formation

Edema

Smooth muscle contraction

Mucous formation

IgE attaches to the surface of mast cell membranes by its Fc fragment. After combining with antigen, vasoactive amines are released from mast cell granules. This increases vascular permeability through endothelial gaps and causes contraction of smooth muscles, specifically those around bronchioles.

Figure 32
Destruction of glomerular basement membrane by a polymorphonuclear leukocyte

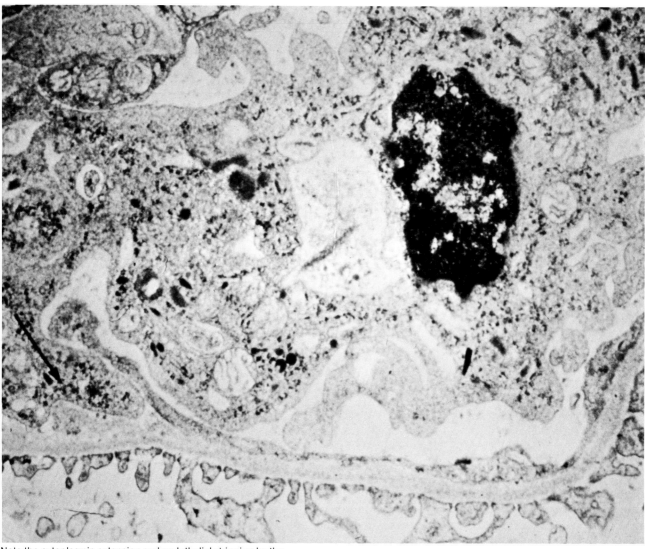

Note the cytoplasmic extension and endothelial stripping by the polymorph.

Reactions Requiring Antibody, Complement, and Polymorphonuclear Leukocytes

The essential role of polymorphonuclear leukocytes (PMNs) in immediate hypersensitivity reactions is best illustrated (Figure 32) by experimental glomerulonephritis that is induced after antibody reacts with the glomerular basement membrane (GBM). The severity of the resultant proteinuria and loss of glomerular ability to retain larger molecular-weight proteins is directly related to the number of PMNs accumulating within the glomerulus. Animals depleted of circulating PMNs do not immediately develop proteinuria following a moderate dose of anti-GBM sufficient to produce proteinuria in animals with normal numbers of PMNs. Transfusion of PMNs into these PMN-depleted animals, however, is followed promptly by glomerular accumulation of PMNs and the onset of proteinuria.

PMNs do not accumulate nor does proteinuria develop if animals are depleted of complement before anti-GBM is given or if the animals are given a form of anti-GBM that does not fix complement. Both lines of evidence indicate that activation of the complement sequence is necessary to cause PMNs to concentrate in the glomerulus. As discussed, C3a, C5a, and C567 are chemotactic for PMNs. Thus, for anti-GBM to injure the glomerulus, complement must be activated so that its chemotactic molecules will attract PMNs that injure the glomerulus (Figure 33).

The lysosomal enzymes of the PMNs cause the glomerular injury. While attempting to phagocytize the bound anti-GBM, PMNs strip away the endothelial lining from the glomerular capillaries that lie in intimate contact with the GBM (Figure 34). During phagocytosis, the PMNs regurgitate some of their lysosomal enzymes. One enzyme, a neutral protease, can degrade GBM in vitro. This probably also occurs in vivo, because large molecular weight GBM fragments are found in the urine of animals with nephritis induced by anti-GBM. The more severe the injury to the GBM, the larger are the proteins in the urine.

The mechanism discussed earlier activates the clotting system, which also plays an important part in the glomerular injury of anti-GBM nephritis. Many studies, both experimental and clinical, indicate that activation of the clotting system provokes proliferation of glomerular endothelial and epithelial cells. Also, glomerular clotting is directly related to later glomerular scarring. Animals treated with anticoagulants, while still developing the immediate effects of anti-GBM nephritis, are spared the proliferative and life-threatening scarring reactions.

Figure 33
Tissue sections stained with FITC-labeled rabbit anti-human immunoglobulin G

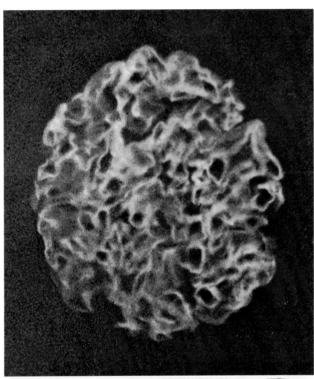

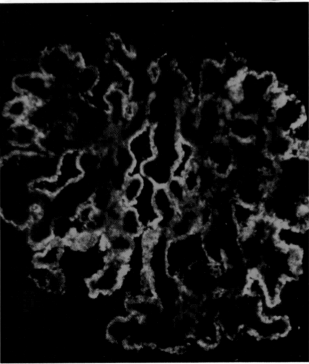

Top: Linear localization of IgG in anti-GBM nephritis. Bottom: Granular or lumpy-bumpy localization of IgG in immune complex nephritis.

Figure 34
**The pathogenesis of antiglomerular basement membrane
nephritis**

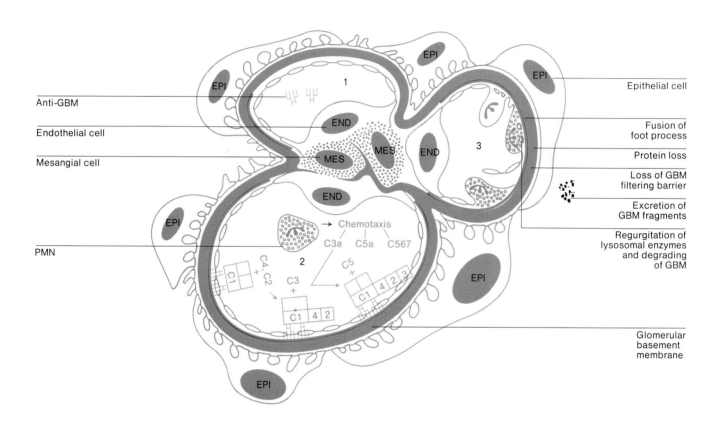

Anti-GBM

Endothelial cell

Mesangial cell

PMN

Epithelial cell

Fusion of
foot process

Protein loss

Loss of GBM
filtering barrier

Excretion of
GBM fragments

Regurgitation of
lysosomal enzymes
and degrading
of GBM

Glomerular
basement
membrane

(1) Circulating anti-GBM combines with glomerular basement
membrane antigens. (2) Following anti-GBM-GBM interaction, the
complement cascade is triggered. Complement sequence activation
leads to the generation of leukocyte chemotactic factors C3a, C5a,
and C567. (3) The attracted PMNs strip away the endothelium and
attempt to phagocytize the anti-GBM and complement bound to the
GBM. During phagocytosis, the PMNs regurgitate lysosomal enzymes,
which begin to degrade the GBM. The degraded GBM loses small
GBM fragments and no longer serves as an effective barrier against
plasma protein loss. In reaction to the filtration of plasma protein, the
foot processes on the epithelial cells fuse, and the GBM is covered by
a continuous sheet of epithelium.

Reactions Requiring Immune Complexes

In this type of immediate hypersensitivity, the cells or injured tissues are innocent bystanders and do not possess antigenic determinants capable of combining with the antibody that initiates the injury. Rather, the antibody reacts with its corresponding soluble antigen present in body fluids, and the resultant circulating immune complex directly or indirectly injures cells or tissues in the vicinity.

In considering how this mechanism destroys erythrocytes and platelets, we should first consider the distinction between fluid-phase and membrane-bound activation. Some activated complement components may exist either free in the fluid phase or bound to membrane receptors or antibody. For example, activated C567 can exist in fluid phase and become attached to nearby cells that are not coated with antibody or earlier complement components. The attached C567 forms a nidus for C8 and C9 uptake and the subsequent lysis of the cell. We should also consider that erythrocytes and platelets also possess membrane receptors for C3b so that immune complexes containing C3b can bind to them. These immune complex-coated cells are also ready targets for the lytic effect of further complement activation and for the macrophages in the reticuloendothelial system.

The mechanism of immune-complex-induced tissue injury is a little more complicated than injury induced in erythrocytes and platelets. Several conditions must be satisfied before the immune complexes can localize within tissues and organs. The immune complex must be of the correct size and must persist in the circulation long enough to localize within tissue. Because large immune complexes are readily phagocytized by the reticuloendothelial system, they do not circulate freely and, therefore, do not have the opportunity to be deposited in tissues. Small molecular weight immune complexes (less than 19S), although they persist in the circulation, are just too small to be deposited in tissue. The size of an immune complex is determined by the ratio of antibody to antigen. Large complexes are formed when antibody is in excess; small ones, when antigen is in excess.

At one time, it was thought that circulating immune complexes of the correct size become localized within the glomerulus because they were trapped by the glomerular filtering action. This hypothesis is now known to be overly simplistic. Instead, the permeability of vessels must first be enhanced before circulating complexes can localize in the extravascular space. Animal studies have demonstrated that during induction of experimental immune complex nephritis, vascular permeability is increased by release of vasoactive amines from their reservoirs, possibly under the influence of IgE.

Thus, if we extrapolate these findings to the serum sickness seen in humans after the administration of horse antitetanus serum, it is apparent that two antibody classes must be formed: conventional IgG antibodies and cytotropic IgE antibodies. The IgG antibody forms circulating immune complexes with the horse serum proteins, whereas the IgE antibody attaches to mast cells and basophils. Reaction of the cell-bound IgE with horse serum causes release of vasoactive amines, and the resultant increased vascular permeability allows circulating immune complexes to localize in the glomerulus of the kidney (Figure 35) and other sites (skin, joints, and heart). Immune complex deposition must occur during the very limited period when the balance between antibody production and concentration of circulating antigens produces the correct antibody-antigen ratio. During the early stages of antibody production, antigen is in excess, and the complexes are small. Later, during full antibody production, antibody is in excess, and the resultant large immune complexes are removed by the reticuloendothelial system. Thus, the symptoms of serum sickness usually appear one to two weeks after the administration of horse serum to a nonsensitized individual.

The glomerular deposition of immune complexes is sufficient to injure the glomerulus and induce proteinuria. At least experimentally, immune complex glomerulonephritis can be produced in complement- and PMN-depleted animals. This is not to say that complement and PMN do not amplify the injury, but they are not absolutely required for the glomerulonephritis. Whether the immune complexes alone or immune complexes plus some unknown effector mechanism produce the glomerular injury awaits further studies. Anti-GBM in very large doses is also capable of initiating glomerular injury without complement or PMN. It is possible that immunologic injury mediated by antibody alone but not mediated by effector systems may be peculiar to the kidney, because the extrarenal manifestations of serum sickness are not seen in animals depleted of complement and/or PMNs.

Figure 35
The pathogenesis of immune complex nephritis

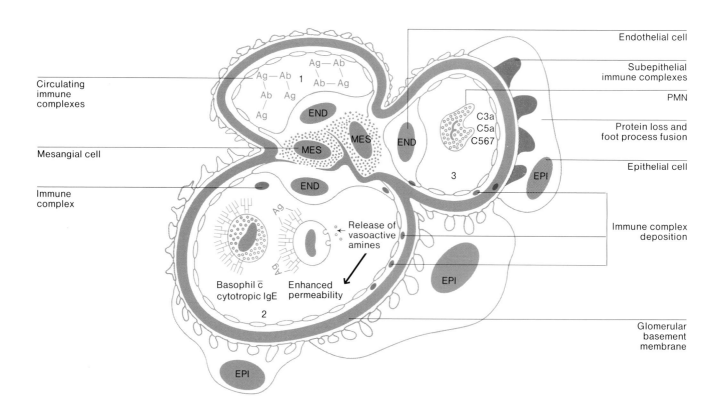

Endothelial cell

Subepithelial
immune complexes

PMN

Protein loss and
foot process fusion

Epithelial cell

Immune complex
deposition

Glomerular
basement
membrane

Circulating
immune
complexes

Mesangial cell

Immune
complex

(1) Immune complexes that are small escape the phagocytic activity of the reticuloendothelial system and persist in the circulation. (2) IgE cytotropic antibody directed against the same antigen circulating in the immune complex is bound to basophils and tissue mast cells by the immunoglobulin's Fc portion. Following antigen interaction with the basophil-bound IgE antibody, the basophil releases its vasoactive amines. The vasoactive amines enhance the permeability of the endothelial lining of the basement membrane. (3) With the enhanced permeability, circulating immune complexes greater than 19S are deposited in the mesangial regions and on the GBM. Glomerular deposition of immune complexes alone is sufficient to promote urinary loss of small molecular weight plasma proteins. Immune complexes through activation of the complement system lead to the production of chemotactic factors that call forth PMNs which, in turn, through their lysosomal enzymes inflict greater damage on the GBM and lead to loss of high molecular weight serum proteins.

Cellular Immunology

4

Two Universes of the Immune Response

Traditionally, in vivo immunologic responses are categorized as immediate hypersensitivity and delayed hypersensitivity (Table 8). An example of an immediate response is the wheal-and-flare reaction that occurs 15 minutes after an extract of ragweed antigen is injected into the skin of a person with hay fever or asthma caused by ragweed. An example of a delayed response is the erythema and induration that occur 24 to 48 hours after tuberculoprotein is injected into the skin of a patient with tuberculosis. A further distinction exists between the universes of immediate and delayed hypersensitivity. The ability to produce these responses can be adoptively conferred upon an immunologically naive recipient. Thus, the ability to give an immediate wheal-and-flare reaction can be transferred to a normal person with serum from a hypersensitive person, whereas delayed hypersensitivity can be transferred with lymphoid cells but not with serum. For these reasons, delayed hypersensitivity is now generally called the universe of cell-mediated immunity (CMI) because it is a property of lymphoid cells. Immediate hypersensitivity is frequently called the universe of antibody-mediated (humoral) hypersensitivity because the antibodies that are present in serum and secretions are responsible for the manifestations of immediate hypersensitivity. Because antibodies (immunoglobulins) are produced by lymphocytes, it is clear that ultimately both universes are dependent upon lymphocyte activities.

Two Classes of Effector Lymphocytes – B and T

Two central lymphoid organs are responsible for the development and maintenance of the two universes. The thymus is responsible for cells participating in the CMI reactions. The central lymphoid organ concerned with the control of antibody-secreting lymphocytes is the bursa of Fabricius in birds and (probably) the bone marrow in mammals. Likewise, there are two families of peripheral lymphoid populations found in the blood, lymph nodes, spleen, and lymphoid tissue of the gastrointestinal and respiratory tracts. The peripheral lymphocytes derived from the bursa of Fabricius (or bone marrow) are called B lymphocytes; those derived from the thymus are called T lymphocytes. The genetics involved in selecting the antibody that a B lymphocyte will produce are described in chapter 1.

Table 8
The two universes of the immune response

	Humoral immunity	Cell-mediated immunity
Rate of response	Minutes – hours	Hours – days
Transferred by	Serum (immunoglobulins)	T lymphocytes
Examples	Anaphylaxis	Tuberculin-type delayed hypersensitivity
	Allergic hay fever and asthma	Allograft rejection
	Bacterial opsonization and lysis	Contact allergy
	Virus and toxin neutralization	Killing of tumor cells
	Immune complex disease	Killing of virus-infected cells
	Some autoimmune phenomena	Some autoimmune phenomena

These lymphoid cell populations are responsible, either directly or indirectly, for the functions of the immune system. They may act alone, but it is more common to see them act together with either of the other lymphocytes of the same (or different) class or with nonlymphocyte accessory cells such as the macrophage. Because of these interactions, the focus of attention in cellular immunology has shifted to the surfaces of the cells involved. Here are located the receptors that govern reactions between cells or between cells and small soluble molecules. In addition, the identification of cell-surface proteins, or markers, helps to distinguish between T cells, B cells, and their subsets.

51

B Lymphocytes and Antibody Formation

Because B-cell function is in some ways less complex than T-cell function, it will be discussed first.

B-cell anatomy and physiology: The bone marrow appears to be the source of cells destined to make antibodies, but it is rarely the locus of large-scale antibody formation. Rather, the bone marrow is the site of intense lymphocyte proliferation that leads to the production of B lymphocytes that quickly leave the marrow and travel to the peripheral lymphoid tissues. There the B lymphocytes may meet an appropriate antigen, become stimulated to divide and differentiate into large lymphocytes and plasma cells, and actively manufacture antibodies.

B lymphocytes are particularly plentiful in areas of antibody production such as the germinal centers of lymph nodes and diffuse lymphoid tissue of the GI and respiratory tracts. They are less common in the blood, rare in the lymph and thoracic duct, and virtually absent from the thymus (Table 9).

Resting B lymphocytes are small lymphocytes typically found in peripheral blood. In fact, they cannot be distinguished from T lymphocytes by conventional light or transmission electron microscopy or (contrary to earlier reports) even by scanning electron microscopy. Therefore, identification of B cells and their distinction from T cells depends on their surface markers as well as their functional properties. Although this differentiation will be discussed later, immunoglobulin is the relevant cell-surface component carried by B lymphocytes.

B-cell receptors and clonal selection: Even before the distinction between B and T cells was known, the clonal selection theory of Talmage and Burnet stated that a lymphocyte destined to make antibody was precommitted to recognize and respond to a limited number of antigens (probably one) – in other words, one lymphocyte, one antibody. Later it was found that, at any time, one lymphocyte could produce antibody of only one immunoglobulin class or subclass, ie, one lymphocyte, one immunoglobulin. Thus, a given B cell can recognize only one antigenic determinant and produce antibody of only one immunoglobulin class. What is the nature of the recognition process? It seems that a mature, resting B lymphocyte (as if it were waiting for the right antigen to appear) has on its surface an immunoglobulin for only one antigen; by this mechanism, the B cell recognizes one antigen and ignores the others. Thus, a B cell, even before activation by antigen, has on its surface membrane a small sample of antibody that it can synthesize when it is properly activated by the appropriate antigen. Other antigens will not specifically interact with these surface immunoglobulins and thus will not activate the B cell.

The presence of immunoglobulin on B cells is generally demonstrated by direct or indirect fluorescence tests using polyvalent antisera to all serum immunoglobulin classes (see chapter 1). However, it is not always easy to identify a particular immunoglobulin on a given B cell. It appears that immature B cells synthesize IgM or IgD (or both), while more mature cells

Table 9
Anatomical locations of T and B lymphocytes

	B lymphocytes	T lymphocytes
Thymus	rare	++++
Bone marrow	++++ (as precursors)	+
Blood	+	+++
Lymph node	++ (germinal centers)	+++ (deep cortex)
Spleen	++	+++
Thoracic duct	+	+++

Table 10
Distinctive surface markers for T and B lymphocytes

T lymphocyte
Theta (Θ) – mouse

Ly antigens – mouse

Receptor for sheep RBC – human

B lymphocyte
Immunoglobulin

Receptor for Fc portion of immunoglobulins

Receptor for activated C3

Figure 36
Dynamics of B-cell surface immunoglobulins

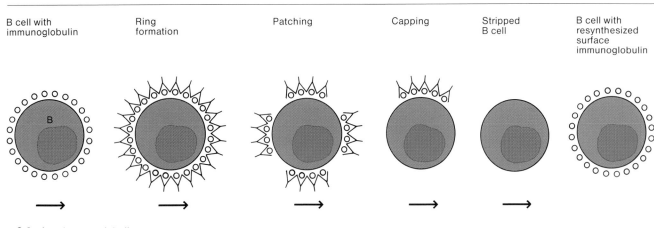

| B cell with immunoglobulin | Ring formation | Patching | Capping | Stripped B cell | B cell with resynthesized surface immunoglobulin |

○ Surface immunoglobulins

➤ Rabbit antihuman immunoglobulin (fluorescein tagged)

Surface immunoglobulins are spread over the surface, but after cross-linking with anti-immunoglobulin, they move into patches, and a cap forms at one pole. This cap is shed (and/or endocytosed), leaving a stripped B cell, which then resynthesizes its surface Ig molecules.

express either IgG, IgA, or IgE. Surface immunoglobulins are diffusely spread over the lymphocyte membrane. The immunoglobulins exist as "islands of protein in a sea of lipid" and thus are mobile in the plane of the membrane, like other proteins in the semifluid membrane. This can be dramatically shown in the following way. Immunofluorescent microscopy shows that resting B cells have surface immunoglobulins in a diffuse or ring form (Figure 36). When cross-linked by anti-immunoglobulin, the surface immunoglobulins coalesce into "patches" and then move into a "cap" over the Golgi apparatus. After that, the cap may be engulfed by endocytosis or may shed (or both); then the surface immunoglobulins regenerate. The relationship between cap formation and triggering of antibody formation is unclear, and the two surface phenomena may be independent.

Although immunoglobulins are the most characteristic B-cell surface markers, macrophages also have immunoglobulins on their surface. However, because immunoglobulins are nonspecifically cytophilic for macrophages, one macrophage may have various classes of immunoglobulins on its surface with different antigenic specificities. Besides immunoglobulins, B cells have other membrane markers, including receptors for the activated third component of complement and for the crystallizable fragment (Fc) portion of immunoglobulins (Table 10).

B-cell activation: The presence of specific antigen receptors on the surfaces of a B lymphocyte helps to explain the clonally restricted nature of antigen recognition. Is the presence of the appropriate antigenic determinant at the surface of the B cell sufficient to activate it to produce quantities of antibody? The question can be restated, "What signals are required to trigger a B cell to produce antibody?" This question has aroused considerable research interest and differences of opinion.

Figure 37
Signals for B lymphocytes

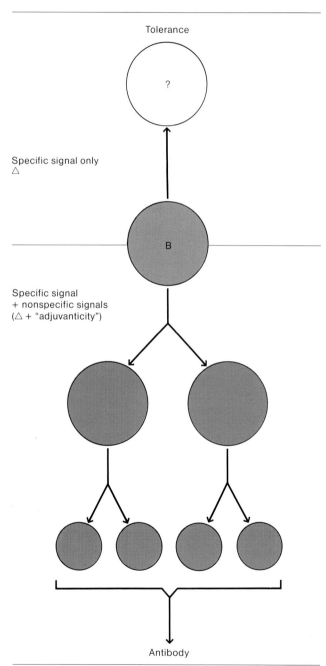

Tolerance

?

Specific signal only
△

B

Specific signal
+ nonspecific signals
(△ + "adjuvanticity")

Antibody

The specific signal alone (△ = antigen) induces tolerance (top). The specific signal (△) plus "adjuvanticity" induces antibody formation (bottom).

Activation by mitogens: There is growing evidence that a B cell requires either a single complex signal (not merely the antigenic determinant) or two separate signals. As mentioned above, the presentation of immunogenic antigen to a clone of B cells results in B-cell activation, differentiation, proliferation, and finally antibody production. However, there are substances called B-cell mitogens that nonspecifically activate all B cells. For example, bacterial endotoxins such as lipopolysaccharide (LPS) have been widely studied in mice. Even in vitro, LPS can nonspecifically "turn on" whole populations of B cells consisting of many clones, and each activated clone will make a very small amount of its appropriate antibody. Although a nonspecific mitogen can indeed activate B cells, such mitogens do not lead to the characteristically large, yet specific, outpouring of antibody that normally follows adequate immunization by a potent antigen.

Activation by antigen: A specific antigen is needed to activate a specific clone of B cells for large-scale antibody production, but the mode of presentation of this antigenic determinant is critical. In fact, there are ways of presenting antigenic signals that do not turn on B-cell clones for antibody production, but rather turn them off, ie, induce tolerance. This tolerance develops particularly with the use of some deaggregated protein antigens and with haptens on nonimmunogenic carriers, which will be discussed later. Therefore, a specific antigenic determinant seems to be necessary but insufficient for vigorous antibody production.

These facts suggest that B cells require two signals for efficient triggering – the specific signal (the antigenic determinant, which it is preprogrammed to recognize) and a nonspecific signal that aids in cell activation, differentiation, and proliferation (Figure 37). Because immunologic adjuvants stimulate antibody production, the second, or nonspecific, signal has been called adjuvanticity.

Triggering B lymphocytes without help: Some antigens seem able to directly trigger B lymphocytes to antibody formation (Figure 38). Although these responses require macrophages (at least in vitro), they do not need the collaboration of T cells (discussed later), and hence are called T independent. These antigens are all polymers and include pneumococcal polysaccharide (soluble), dextran (polyglucose), levan (polyfructose), polyvinylpyrrolidone (PVP), LPS, and others. The antibody responses to these polymers are peculiar in that they yield IgM almost exclusively, produce little or no "memory," and readily induce tolerance. Because T lymphocytes may be involved in helper (or second signal) activity, how do these T-independent antigens fit in with the idea that it takes two signals to trigger a B cell? Again, there is controversy on this point, but it seems that each T-independent antigen is also a general B-cell mitogen and, therefore, carries its own adjuvanticity. In other words, each PVP molecule, for example, carries both the specific and nonspecific signals needed for triggering antibody formation. However, the intrinsic adjuvanticity of these soluble T-independent antigens is weak, and antibody responses to them can be boosted with additional extrinsic adjuvanticity, eg, LPS, playing its role as a nonspecific B-cell mitogen. In addition, macrophages can also provide adjuvanticity.

Triggering B lymphocytes with help: Most antigens are not simple polymers but instead include microorganisms, proteins, glycoproteins, and haptens on various carriers. These complex antigens may induce immunoglobulin G, E, A, and M responses, produce memory, but do not induce tolerance. The antibody responses to these antigens are *thymus dependent* because the B cells require T-cell help. As a result, animals deprived of T cells, eg, by neonatal thymectomy or by adult thymectomy followed by irradiation and B-cell reconstitution with bone marrow and congenitally thymus-deprived (nude) mice, respond little or not at all to these antigens.

Numerous experiments have not elucidated the mechanism of T-cell help, mainly because we do not know the nature of the T-cell receptor for antigen (a topic discussed later). Regardless of the nature of this receptor, however, the clonal restriction of T cells implies that they do have some type of antigen-specific receptors.

The antigen bridge model: The early *antigen-bridge* model (Figure 39) reconciled the observation that, in hapten-carrier systems, T cells recognized the carrier whereas B cells recognized the hapten. The B cell then made antihapten antibody. Also, in these systems, the hapten and the carrier had to be on the same molecule. It was believed that T cells in some fashion focused the complex antigen attached to the carrier portion and presented the appropriate B cell with a matrix of hapten determinants that could activate the B lymphocyte.

Figure 38
Triggering B lymphocytes without help

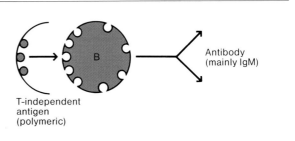

T-independent antigen (polymeric)

Antibody (mainly IgM)

Under certain circumstances, B lymphocytes can be triggered for antibody production without T-cell help. In these cases, the antigens are polymeric and appear to provide their own adjuvanticity.

Figure 39
Triggering B cells with T-cell help

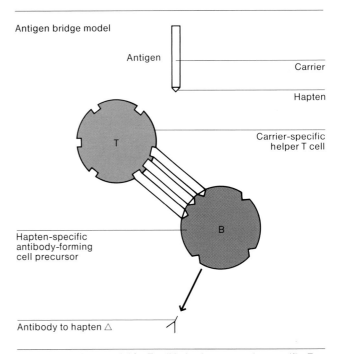

Antigen bridge model

Antigen

Carrier

Hapten

Carrier-specific helper T cell

Hapten-specific antibody-forming cell precursor

Antibody to hapten △

The antigen bridge model for T-cell help shows a carrier-specific, T-cell focusing antigen, so that the B cell is presented with a matrix array of haptenic determinants (△).

T-cell factors: Later it was recognized that T-helper cells were actively involved in helping (Figure 40) rather than passively *focusing* antigen. Furthermore, T- and B-cell collaboration could be demonstrated even when the cells were separated by a cell-impermeable membrane, implying that collaboration required transfer of a soluble substance. At present, the nature of T-cell help is not completely clarified. However, evidence shows that populations of T lymphocytes produce nonspecific soluble factors when they are stimulated with T-cell mitogens, such as phyto-hemagglutinin (PHA) or concanavalin A (con A). Together with specific antigen (the first signal), these nonspecific factors appear to act as the second signal in triggering B cells precommitted to that antigen (Figure 40a). The adjuvant effect of nonspecific T-cell stimuli can also be seen in the *allogeneic effect* that results when mixtures of allogeneic cells, ie, cells with different histocompatibility antigens, stimulate each other to produce nonspecific T-cell products. These products, as well as other substances such as LPS, can substitute for antigen-activated specific T-cells (Figure 40b, Table 11). That is, nonspecific T-cell products plus antigen can trigger B-cell responses in the absence of T cells.

There is also evidence that antigen-stimulated T cells can produce antigen-specific soluble factors. These factors resemble immunoglobulins but differ from conventional antibodies. They may be a special class of T-cell products, perhaps the T-cell antigen receptors. In the hapten-carrier system, this model visualizes T cells as being stimulated by their specific carrier antigen and then releasing the carrier-specific factor. This factor, together with the complete antigen (hapten carrier), forms a complex that is arrayed on the surface of a macrophage. The macrophage then "presents" the hapten to the appropriate B lymphocyte, which is triggered to make antihapten antibody (Figure 40a).

Figure 40
Two models showing T-cell help for B-cell activation

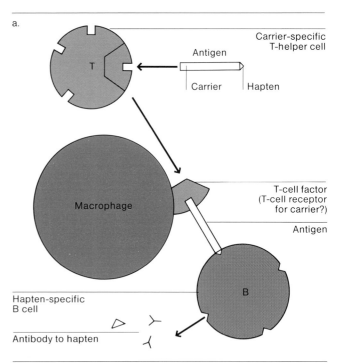

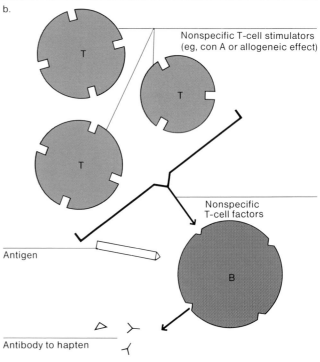

The upper part shows the help in the form of a specific T-cell factor induced by antigen. The lower part shows the help in the form of nonspecific T-cell factors induced by nonspecific T-cell stimulators.

Table 11
Summary of signal theory for B-cell triggering

	First signal	Second signal
T-independent antigens	Antigen A	Antigen as mitogen? (Figure 38)
T-dependent antigens (considered as hapten carrier)	a) Hapten	*T-cell "help"* either from (1) antigen bridge which focuses hapten (Figure 39)
		(2) T-cell factor from carrier-stimulated T cell (Figure 40a)
		(3) factor from T cells stimulated by other antigens (eg, allo-genic cells) (Figure 40b)
	b) Hapten	*B-cell mitogen* acting without T cells

Macrophages and Antigen Presentation

Lymphocytes and macrophages seem to have an affinity for each other, and both are involved in antibody formation, but their respective functions are not clear. A common opinion was that macrophages *digested* complex antigens to make them *palatable* for B cells. Another concept was that macrophages ingested antigen and then manufactured some informational type of ribonucleic acid (RNA) that (with or without antigen) was transferred to a B lymphocyte to trigger it into antibody formation. While both concepts are still viable, attention has shifted to the macrophage surface membrane to help explain why macrophage-associated antigen is so highly immunogenic for T lymphocytes.

The exact mechanism by which macrophages present antigen to T cells or B cells is under investigation, but two important questions remain unanswered. One involves how interaction between the genetically coded cell-surface molecules of the major histocompatibility complex (MHC) on the surface of the macrophage, in association with antigen, determines the effectiveness of lymphocyte triggering. Another problem involves the nature and mode of action of soluble products produced by macrophages that modulate antibody responses.

T Lymphocytes and Cell-Mediated Immunity

Besides antibody-mediated hypersensitivity, there is the other universe of immune responses – cell-mediated immunity (CMI) or delayed hypersensitivity that involves T lymphocytes.

T-cell anatomy and physiology: The thymus manufactures large numbers of T lymphocytes at about the same rate as the bone marrow produces B lymphocytes. Thymocytes are created by rapid cell division in the thymus cortex, but their mitotic rate slows as they move toward the medulla. Before or after reaching the medulla, these T cells (now almost mature) migrate into the bloodstream, where they comprise about 60% of the peripheral blood lymphocytes. In the bloodstream, they follow a unique pattern of recirculation – from blood to lymph node to thoracic duct and back to blood (Figure 41). While in the lymph node, most T lymphocytes reside in the deep cortex and areas between germinal centers – the so-called *thymic-dependent* areas, which are not in the germinal centers where B cells are. Some T cells go from blood to spleen and back to blood, while a small number gain access to the bone-marrow compartment. This pool of mature T lymphocytes is often called the recirculating pool of long-lived T lymphocytes, and some of these resting cells have been shown to live for over 20 years without dividing. Thus, the thymus appears to *seed* the peripheral lymphoid tissues with a supply of mature long-lived T cells. One would correctly predict that thymectomy in an adult would not drastically affect this peripheral T-cell pool for some time.

Nevertheless, there are some cycling and short-lived T cells in the peripheral lymphoid tissues, particularly in the spleen. They probably include (among other cells) the precursors of suppressor T cells (discussed later) that seem to be under somewhat closer to thymic control than are the long-lived peripheral T cells. As might be expected, thymectomy in the adult affects this population sooner than it affects the long-lived pool. We do not know whether thymectomy affects this population by removing the source of precursor cells or by cutting off the supply of some thymic hormone.

Figure 41
T-lymphocyte production and circulation

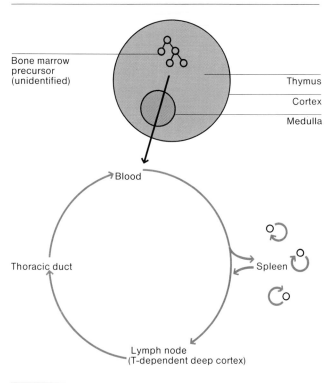

Bone marrow
precursor
(unidentified)

Thymus

Cortex

Medulla

Blood

Thoracic duct

Spleen

Lymph node
(T-dependent deep cortex)

T lymphocytes are produced by rapid mitosis in the thymic cortex. They migrate into the medulla, slowing down their mitotic rate. Some leave the thymus in a nondividing state to enter the blood, forming the long-lived pool of recirculating T lymphocytes. There are some short-lived peripheral T lymphocytes, as shown by the cycling symbol in the spleen.

T-cell surface markers: T cells have distinctive surface markers that help distinguish them from B cells. Unlike B cells, T cells do not have surface immunoglobulins that can be detected by fluorescence microscopy using anti-Ig reagents. In a positive sense, T cells also have surface components not shared by B cells (Table 10).

T-cell identification in the mouse has been greatly aided by the discovery of a surface antigen called *theta* (Θ). By using an antiserum to the theta antigen (anti-Θ), one can identify T cells in mixed lymphocyte populations by immunofluorescence. Also, one can deplete lymphocyte populations of their T cells by treatment with anti-Θ plus complement. Furthermore, using anti-Θ, it was shown that antigen is present in different concentrations on the T-cell membrane at different times in the life of the cell. Quantitation of Θ antigen serves as an index of cell maturation, and for this reason, Θ can be considered a true differentiation marker. For example, Θ is very rich on the surface of thymus cortex lymphocytes, less concentrated on more mature thymus medullary lymphocytes, and still less concentrated on peripheral T cells. There is evidence that a few T cells in the bone marrow have virtually no Θ antigen.

In man, a counterpart to the mouse Θ antigen has not been completely defined. Nevertheless, in vitro human T lymphocytes can be rapidly counted because sheep red blood cells (SRBC) adhere to them (Figure 42). Therefore, upon mixing a suspension of human peripheral blood cells with a suspension of SRBC, 60% to 70% of the lymphocytes are surrounded by an SRBC rosette. Other criteria indicate that the human lymphocytes that form rosettes with SRBC are thymus-derived cells. Thus, by using the SRBC rosette method to count T lymphocytes and fluorescent antisera to surface immunoglobulins to identify B lymphocytes, one can account for the majority of human lymphocytes. However, the SRBC rosette method is not a functional test; it identifies T cells but does not indicate their functional capabilities. Functional tests for T lymphocytes exist, such as stimulation by the T-cell mitogens (PHA or con A), stimulation by specific antigens, or ability to participate in mixed lymphocyte reactions. These tests are covered in chapter 5.

Figure 42
Human T-cell rosettes

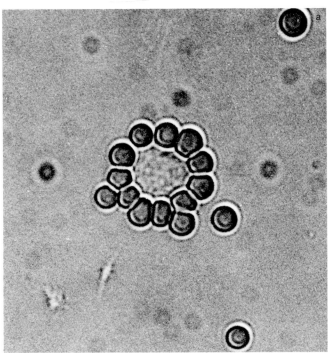
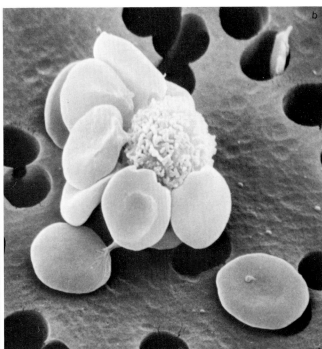

a. A human T lymphocyte surrounded by sheep erythrocytes as seen in a hemocytometer.

b. A similar cell as seen in the scanning electron microscope.

T-cell receptor for antigen: In recent years, one of the most vigorous controversies in cellular immunology concerned the nature of receptors used by T cells to recognize antigen. Although B cells use surface immunoglobulin for this purpose, a number of investigators failed to find immunoglobulin on T cells. Still, the possibility existed that T cells had another library of diverse antigen receptors that were not immunoglobulins. Further complications arose because some experiments detected immunoglobulins on T cells. Finally, the situation was resolved by the finding that T cells have antigen receptors that resemble immunoglobulins. These molecules are coded by genes responsible for the V_H region of immunoglobulin heavy chains, but they are not conventional serum immunoglobulins.

Immunogenetics and T-cell recognition: Another important finding is that T cells recognize antigen only in the context of the MHC. Although this topic is extremely complicated and cannot be discussed in detail here, some superficial understanding of the situation is essential.

A simplified version of the mouse MHC shows two genetic regions that code for histocompatibility antigens, the K series on the left end and the D series on the right (Figure 43). These regions are separated by the I region (for *immune* response) in the middle. It is now clear that the T-cell receptor is complex and recognizes an antigen, eg, a viral antigen on a cell surface), only if the T cell has the same specificity in the MHC (usually K or D) region as the infected cell. But how is such recognition achieved? Does the T cell have

Figure 43
Diagram of the major histocompatibility genetic regions of mouse and man

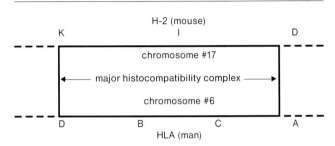

The I region (immune response region) in the mouse corresponds to the HLA-D region in man. Mouse K and D regions correspond to human B and A regions.

two receptors – one for the MHC region and one for the antigen? Or does the T cell have a receptor that recognizes an altered-self antigen, ie, one formed by a modification of the MHC by the antigen? The function of the I region, on the other hand, is at least twofold. It codes for products (as yet unknown) that somehow determine whether the organism will respond vigorously to an antigen (ie, as a *responder*), or poorly, or not at all (ie, a *nonresponder*). Also, I-region coded molecules on macrophages assume importance in antigen presentation to T cells.

These problems are being solved in the mouse; however, it is clear that the MHC of man (including the HLA system) also controls immunoregulatory processes. An understanding of this area is crucial in the fields of transplantation and autoimmunity and will be explored rapidly (see chapter 8).

T-Cell Activation

Like B cells, T cells can be activated by several stimuli.

Activation by mitogens: T cells can be activated by a variety of mitogenic substances that cause resting T cells to synthesize RNA, protein, and DNA, leading to the development of large lymphoblasts that may then divide. This results in polyclonal, or nonspecific, activation of a large fraction of T cells, regardless of their antigenic specificity. The most widely used mitogens are phytohemagglutinin (PHA) and concanavalin A (con A). The ability of cultures of animal or human cells to respond to these mitogens is semiquantitative functional test of T-cell activity. As will be discussed later, such activated T cells also release soluble factors.

Activation by specific antigen: T cells are clonally restricted and respond to one antigen (or a close relative of it) when the antigen reacts with the T-cell receptor under certain circumstances. This stimulation occurs when that antigen is presented by the macrophage membrane. Next the T-cell clone multiplies by cell division and maturation, and effector T cells appear. These effector cells manifest T-cell function in a variety of ways:

a. Helper T cells (T_h). These cells, described above, *help* B cells make antibody to thymus-dependent antigens.

b. Suppressor T cells (T_s). These T cells are responsible for *down-regulation* of immune responses, and they generally inhibit Th or other T amplifier cells (discussed later).

c. Cytotoxic T cells (T_C). T_C cells kill antigen-modified self-cells or allogeneic cells after direct contact. They are probably important in transplantation and tumor immunity.

d. Delayed hypersensitivity T cells (T_{DH}). These specialized cells may be similar to T_C but are involved in delayed hypersensitivity reactions such as contact sensitivity. They promote inflammation by releasing soluble factors.

T-cell cooperation and diversity: It seems that T cells often work together with other T cells. Recently, amplifier T cells that increase the responses of the other cells have been discovered; such complex cellular interactions are important in immunoregulation.

In the early days of T-cell study, it was believed that a single class of T cells existed, but when studied under various conditions, they manifested different functions. We now know, however, that separate subclasses of T cells are responsible for different effector functions. This differentiation has been helped by the discovery of markers for T-cell subsets, the lymphocyte T (LyT) system. Helper T cells (Th) and T cells for delayed hypersensitivity (T_{DH}) carry the LyT-1 markers and suppressor T cells (Ts), and cytotoxic T cells (Tc) bear the LyT-2,3 markers.

T-cell effector mechanisms: We are not certain how different T cells exert their effects. Some appear to work by direct interaction with their targets (eg, cytotoxic T cells) and others liberate specific soluble factors (eg, suppressor T cells). As discussed, it is not clear whether T-helper cells directly influence B cells by the antigen bridge or whether they release a soluble helper factor. However, it is clear that T cells responsible for delayed hypersensitivity (T_{DH}) release a variety of soluble factors (eg, migration inhibition factor) that are responsible for their effects.

Immunoregulation

A question of great interest to immunologists is, "How is the immune response regulated?" This raises fundamental questions: (1) What limits the response in a dynamic system such as the immune response in which amplification of T- and B-cell populations occur? (2) If autoimmune phenomena are manifestations of the failure of self-tolerance, what mechanisms are awry? (3) If people of certain genetic backgrounds are unusually susceptible (or resistant) to certain diseases, microorganisms, or tumors, what regulatory mechanisms control their immune responses? (4) How does one dampen unwanted immune responses (transplantation rejection or allergic reactions) and stimulate flagging ones (immunodeficiency)?

Natural regulation and the network theory: There is evidence that *natural* regulatory circuits are built into the immunologic system and modify the immune response. These include negative feedback by an antibody to reduce further antibody production and suppression of T-cell functions by T_S. Even more intriguing is Jerne's hypothesis of an immunologic *network*. This regulatory system maintains a balance between lymphocyte receptors for antigen (the idiotypes) and cells or antibodies that are directed against these cell receptors (ie, anti-idiotypes). Antigen perturbs the system and amplifies the idiotype-bearing cells (and thus the T- and B-cell responses). These responses set off their own antigen-specific, anti-idiotype reactions that dampen the system and return it to the original, or a new, steady state. This fascinating idea is now being widely explored.

Immunologic unresponsiveness and tolerance: Of great practical importance is the question: How does one deliberately induce unresponsiveness to a specific antigen? This question deals with the problems of transplantation rejection and autoimmunity that can be seen as unwanted recognition of nonself and unwanted nonrecognition of self, respectively. We now know that unresponsiveness can be established in a variety of ways, and no single mechanism can explain all the observed phenomena. Several mechanisms may be involved: (1) the results of direct interaction between the antigen used to induce tolerance and the immunocompetent lymphocytes (T and B) that lead (without "help") to clone deletion or abortion, blockade of the receptor for antigen, and exhaustion of the clone by excess immunization. Unresponsiveness may be accomplished using antigens that evade macrophage processing such as some deaggregated globulins, antigens on self-carriers, or antigens on nonimmunogenic polymers; (2) indirect effects upon immunocompetent lymphocytes by blocking antibodies (antiantigen and antireceptor [anti-idiotype]), suppressor cells, and suppressor factors.

This complex situation is being rapidly explored to provide better methods of controlling immune responses when the network seems to have failed.

Selected Bibliography

Broder S, Waldmann TA: The suppressor-cell network in cancer. *N Engl J Med 299*:1281, 1978.

Paul WE, Benacerraf B: Functional specificity of thymus-dependent lymphocytes. *Science 195*:1293, 1977.

Rowlands DT, Daniele RP: Surface receptors in the immune response. *N Engl J Med 293*: 26, 1975.

Delayed Hypersensitivity and Immunodeficiency

Introduction

One of the earliest immunologic reactions recorded, the phenomenon of delayed, or cellular, hypersensitivity, was described in 1801 by Jenner, who noted the "disposition to sudden cuticular inflammation" that occurred after cowpox had been reinoculated into the skin of persons previously vaccinated by cowpox or infected with smallpox virus. Ninety years later, Koch, in his studies on experimental tuberculosis, emphasized that this modified reaction to an infectious agent is brought about by previous exposure. He observed that the inoculation of cultures of bacilli into a tuberculous guinea pig created an inflamed area after one or two days, whereas little reaction occurred in normal animals similarly injected until 10 to 14 days later. The *Koch phenomenon* could be elicited by living or dead tubercle bacilli as well as by old tuberculin (a glycerin broth culture of mycobacteria, concentrated and freed of bacilli by filtration). This phenomenon is the model of delayed hypersensitivity reactions (Figure 44) and is the basis for the tuberculin test that uses purified protein derivative of tuberculin (PPD).

Definition of Delayed Hypersensitivity

When an antigen is injected intradermally into an appropriately sensitized individual, an inflammatory reaction ensues that reaches its peak within 24 to 48 hours. The reaction consists mainly of erythema and induration (Figure 44) and is called delayed hypersensitivity to differentiate it from immediate hypersensitivity, or Arthus, reactions.

The immediate reactions depend directly upon antibody and are transferred easily to nonsensitized animals by antibody-containing serum. If reaginic antibody (IgE) is present, a reaction will develop within minutes of injection of the antigen. If precipitin antibodies are present, an Arthus reaction appears after two hours. Precipitin antibodies may precipitate antigen in either in vivo or various in vitro tests. In contrast, reactions of delayed hypersensitivity are unrelated to conventional circulating antibody and are regularly transferred passively from sensitized to normal animals with immunocompetent cells (lymphocytes) but not with serum. This close association of delayed hypersensitivity with cells rather than serum antibody sets the phenomenon apart from other immune reactions.

Figure 44
Positive delayed hypersensitivity skin test

Note swelling and erythema.

Delayed Hypersensitivity Manifestations

Although local dermal reactions of delayed hypersensitivity have been extensively studied, there are also other manifestations. In a hypersensitive individual, a systemic reaction will occur if a sufficient quantity of tuberculin is absorbed into the bloodstream. The symptoms include fever, malaise, backache, and pain in the joints, accompanied by a depression of monocytes; when the reaction is severe, shock and death may occur. Although small amounts of tuberculin can elicit such responses in hypersensitive individuals, a nonsensitive person can tolerate many thousand times as much tuberculin without a systemic reaction. Several factors may be involved in this complicated reaction; the individuals not only exhibit delayed hypersensitivity but may also have circulating antibody. Also, such individuals may be hypersensitive to endotoxin, a material that is frequently found in bacterial preparations. The fever and depression of monocytes following systemic tuberculin injection are manifestations of delayed hypersensitivity, whereas the shock can result from the effect of antibody or endotoxin.

How Delayed Hypersensitivity Is Established

Microorganisms: Delayed hypersensitivity may occur following infections with numerous organisms, eg, the tubercle bacilli. Bacteria such as *Brucella* and the typhoid bacillus, which cause chronic infection and granulomas and which multiply inside host cells, are also good inducers of this type of sensitivity. Following streptococcal, pneumococcal, and diphtherial infections, delayed hypersensitivity has developed, but it is not directly involved in the progress and pathogenesis of these acute bacterial diseases. Delayed hypersensitivity has also been observed after viral, fungal, protozoal, and other parasitic infections. Also, the granulomas seen around *Schistosoma mansoni* eggs are due in part to delayed hypersensitivity reactions to egg antigen.

Proteins: Although delayed hypersensitivity was first thought to be limited to the infectious process and was referred to as bacterial allergy, similar reactions can be elicited by nonbacterial proteins. To experimentally induce delayed hypersensitivity in animals, protein antigens are emulsified with complete adjuvant; the combination elicits a more potent immune response than does the protein alone. The adjuvant is usually a suspension of dead tubercle bacilli in oil; but other organisms, such as *Nocardia*, can substitute for mycobacteria. Considerable work is being carried out to develop adjuvants safe for use in man. Promising candidates include muramyldipeptide (MDP), an active ingredient from mycobacteria, as well as synthetic derivatives of MDP. Other substances isolated from mycobacteria and *Nocardia* are being tested as well. Another method of enhancing the immune response is to incorporate antigen and adjuvant into lipid envelopes called liposomes. Further, conjugation of protein antigens with certain lipids enhances delayed hypersensitivity reactions to the protein but diminishes the antibody response. Despite extensive research, the mechanism of adjuvant action is not known; adjuvant may enhance T-cell helper function.

Proteins also induce delayed hypersensitivity when injected repeatedly into the skin, either as antigen-antibody complexes or as proteins alone. Since many basophils are present in lesions produced in this manner, the reaction is referred to as cutaneous basophilic hypersensitivity.

Chemicals: Another form of delayed hypersensitivity can be induced by applying simple chemicals to the skin (Figures 45 and 46). In man, the most common example of such contact sensitivity is poison ivy contact dermatitis. Experimentally, picryl chloride and 2,4-dinitrochlorobenzene (DNCB) have been extensively used to study this type of sensitivity. Under these conditions, a small chemical group (hapten) binds to a skin protein via a free amino or sulfhydryl group. The hapten-protein conjugate induces or elicits this type of sensitivity. This was the first form of delayed hypersensitivity to be transferred to an unsensitized animal by injecting cells from a sensitized animal. Significant basophilic infiltration has recently been described in lesions of hypersensitivity induced by chemicals.

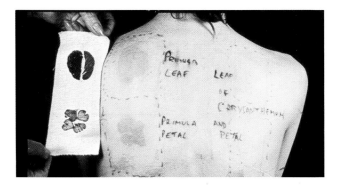

Figure 45
Contact sensitivity to a plant leaf

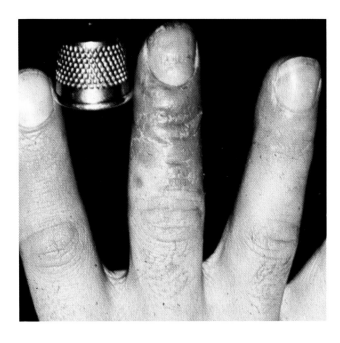

Figure 46
Contact sensitivity to a sewing thimble

Route of sensitization: The route of sensitization also is important in the induction of delayed hypersensitivity. For example, subcutaneous injection of streptococci induces delayed hypersensitivity, but injection of the same bacteria intravenously induces antibody production without delayed hypersensitivity. Indeed, intravenous injection of antigen may temporarily desensitize an individual to the specific antigen injected or may induce the production of suppressor T cells. This may explain why some patients with miliary tuberculosis lose their delayed hypersensitivity – presumably during bacillemia. Further, proteins conjugated to cells and injected subcutaneously will induce delayed hypersensitivity to the protein. However, if the same protein-cell conjugate is injected intravenously, the delayed hypersensitivity response is suppressed because suppressor T cells are induced. Antigens injected into the skin are more likely to produce delayed hypersensitivity than those given intravenously, which may explain why drug sensitivity is more common after topical administration of medication.

Immunologic Specificity
Studies with haptens conjugated to proteins, with denatured proteins, and with isolated peptides have greatly increased our understanding of immunologic specificity in general and of the specificity of delayed hypersensitivity in particular. It appears that protein antigens must be presented to the T cell by a macrophage. The macrophage probably processes the antigen to some extent, since denatured proteins induce a delayed hypersensitivity that cross-reacts with native proteins. However, the B cell appears to recognize the tertiary structure of the protein, because denatured proteins induce antibodies that do not react with the native protein. On the other hand, the use of haptens, eg, dinitrophenol (DNP), illustrates another difference between the specificity of the T-cell receptor and that of humoral antibody. If dinitrophenol (DNP) that is conjugated to guinea-pig albumin is injected into the guinea pig with mycobacteria and oil as adjuvant, the animal produces antibodies that interact predominantly with the DNP group, whether the hapten is attached to guinea-pig albumin or to another unrelated protein. That is, the antibody is specific for the hapten. However, to elicit delayed hypersensitivity in this case, DNP must be conjugated to guinea-pig albumin, the

same carrier protein used for sensitization. If the hapten is conjugated to an unrelated protein, it will not elicit delayed reactions in vivo or in vitro. Thus, the antigenic determinant recognized by the T-cell receptor involves both the hapten and part of the carrier protein. This phenomenon is referred to as hapten-carrier protein specificity. If, on the other hand, DNP is coupled to carriers that induce antibody without the need of T cells, such as DNP-Ficoll or DNP-mycobacteria, it will induce a hapten-specific delayed hypersensitivity that appears to be B-cell dependent.

Studies using small synthetic antigens show a relationship between the immunogenic properties of a molecule and its ability to elicit delayed reactions. A chain of seven or more lysines is required for a DNP-polypeptide to be an immunogen, that is, able to sensitize an animal to produce antibodies. Similarly, the antigen must have seven or more lysines attached to DNP to elicit the delayed reaction either in vivo or in vitro. Although DNP-oligopeptide that contains as few as three or four lysines reacts with preformed antibody, it cannot act as an immunogen or elicit delayed hypersensitivity.

In summary, the T cell recognizes a small part of the carrier protein plus the hapten; the antigenic determinant is thought to combine with Ia antigen on the macrophage. Either the B cell or circulating antibody recognizes the tertiary structure of the protein or, when hapten-protein conjugates are used, mainly the hapten.

Delayed Hypersensitivity: A Thymus-Dependent System

Studies in the chicken emphasize the duality of the immune response. This animal has two primary immune organs: the thymus and the bursa of Fabricius (Figure 47). If the bursa is removed, the chicken develops a serious deficiency in antibody production but maintains normal cellular immune reactions, as assessed by the rejection of skin grafts and the exhibition of delayed hypersensitivity. However, if the thymus is removed, the cellular immune mechanism is depressed while the antibody process continues.

Immunologic deficiency diseases in man show a similar duality. However, in mammals, primary immune organs (other than the thymus) have not yet been clearly defined, although the equivalent of the bursa of Fabricius is now thought to be the bone marrow.

Figure 47
Central lymphoid tissue of the two primary immune organs in the chicken

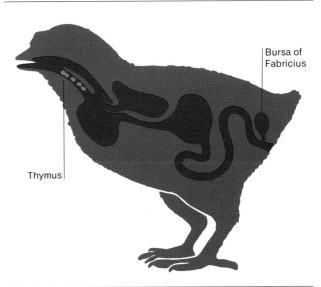

Bursa of Fabricius

Thymus

The bursa of Fabricius controls the development of antibody production. The thymus determines cellular immune reactivity by peripheral lymphoid tissues.

Lymph Node and Cellular Hypersensitivity

From the immunologic viewpoint, the lymph node areas of greatest interest are the germinal follicles and paracortical areas (Figure 48). The germinal follicles grow rapidly when antigens that stimulate antibodies are administered to an animal, and increased numbers of plasma cells appear in the node. On the other hand, the paracortical regions are especially affected when a chemical known to induce cellular hypersensitivity (eg, dinitrochlorobenzene) is placed on the skin draining to that node. In addition to paracortical enlargement, many pyroninophilic mononuclear cells, which contain increased amounts of ribonucleic acid (RNA), are seen. Many of these cells later develop into small lymphocytes.

The relationship of the lymph node's paracortical region to cellular hypersensitivity has been emphasized. For example, thymectomy in mice decreases the size of paracortical areas and diminishes the cellular response. Antilymphocyte sera, which act predominantly on the cellular immune system rather than on the antibody system, markedly alter the paracortical areas but not the germinal centers of lymph nodes. Also, some patients with lepromatous leprosy, who are anergic and do not exhibit delayed hypersensitivity, have very sparse paracortical areas in their nodes, but those exhibiting good dermal hypersensitivity have normal paracortical areas (Figures 49 and 50).

Transfer of Delayed Hypersensitivity

Unlike other immune reactions, delayed hypersensitivity cannot be passively transferred from sensitive to normal animals using serum, but viable cells from peritoneal exudates, lymph nodes, or spleens can transfer the reaction. Transfer of sensitivity is detected as early as 24 hours after injection of sensitive cells into a normal guinea pig. Sensitivity usually lasts about one week, then disappears because the sensitive cells are presumably removed by a homograft reaction in a histoincompatible host. This explains why transfers between inbred guinea pigs greatly prolong sensitivity because the donor cells survive longer in the histocompatible host. The exact mechanism of the transferred sensitivity is still not known. However, the transfer lasts only one week in randomly bred guinea pigs but much longer in inbred animals, which suggests that the sensitive cells are acting directly rather than by transferring information to host cells.

Although delayed hypersensitivity has been transferred between strains of guinea pigs that are not completely histocompatible, in mice the recipient of the sensitized cells must have the same Ia haplotype as the donor cells before delayed hypersensitivity to protein antigens is exhibited after transfer. On the other hand, transfer of contact sensitivity in mice (eg, dinitrofluorobenzene) requires that the recipient and the donor must be histocompatible either at the I region or the K and D regions (see chapter 6).

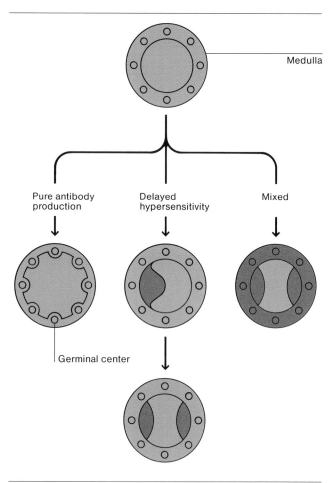

Figure 48
Lymph node reaction to antigenic stimulation

■ Paracortical area

An antigen that stimulates primarily a cellular immune response induces cellular proliferation in the paracortical area of the lymph node. An antigen that stimulates antibody production affects only the development of prominent germinal centers.

Figure 49
Morphology of lymph node

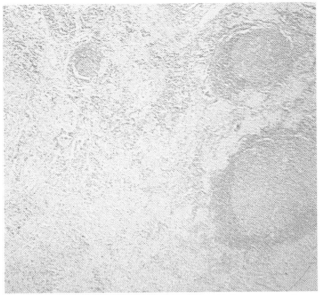

With marked anergy and no delayed hypersensitivity response, the paracortical areas of the lymph nodes are sparse.

Figure 50
Morphology of lymph node

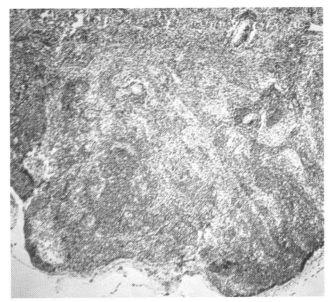

With good delayed hypersensitivity, the paracortical regions are normal.

How transferred cells act: When ³H-thymidine-labeled cells from sensitive donors are injected into normal recipients, there is no preferential accumulation of labeled cells at the site of a skin test with either the antigen to which the donor was sensitive or a different antigen. Accumulation of labeled cells at these sites averages only 4% of the total number of cells reaching the site, and the majority of cells at the test site are nonsensitive. When nonlabeled sensitive cells are injected into normal animals whose cells had been previously labeled by ³H-thymidine, 68% to 91% of the cells at the test site are labeled. The majority of infiltrating cells are normal, nonsensitive host cells derived from blood monocytes that originate from the bone marrow. Thus, a few sensitive cells may reach the site at random, interact with antigen, and set off a reaction that involves a larger number of nonsensitive cells.

Transfer of delayed hypersensitivity involves more than just specifically sensitive cells. Guinea pigs deprived of vitamin C do not express delayed hypersensitivity; however, cells from sensitized scorbutic animals can transfer delayed hypersensitivity to normal recipients. The normal donor is essential because sensitive cells from nonscorbutic animals fail to transfer sensitivity to nonsensitized scorbutic guinea pigs. Thus, the dermal-delayed hypersensitivity response can be depressed – despite the presence of sensitive cells.

How specifically sensitive cells act after transfer is not known. Studies show that in the guinea pig the cells must be capable of active metabolism, which argues against the mediation of delayed hypersensitivity by preformed cell factors. Further, transfer of delayed hypersensitivity is inhibited when sensitive cells are incubated with mitomycin, which prevents cell division prior to transfer. The necessity for intact metabolizing cells in order to effect transfer in the guinea pig is in marked contrast to the situation in humans.

Figure 51
Delayed hypersensitivity reaction

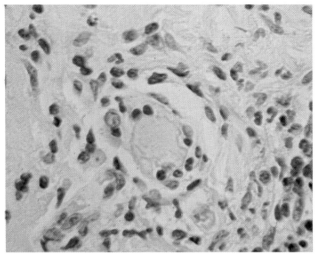

Mononuclear cells accumulate around a small blood vessel.

Transfer of delayed hypersensitivity in humans: Transfer of delayed hypersensitivity in humans requires either peripheral blood leukocytes or extracts of these cells. Studies using ethylene oxide-treated human serum – an antigen that does not induce detectable antibody in the host – show that it is possible to transfer delayed hypersensitivity to subjects not skin tested before transfer, thus obviating any role of skin testing itself. The transfer of sensitivity to keyhole-limpet hemocyanin (KLH) without prior skin testing has also been reported.

Transfer factor: The factor responsible for these delayed reactions is obtained by alternate freezing and thawing of peripheral white blood cells from sensitive donors and treating with deoxyribonuclease (DNase) to reduce the viscosity of the extract. The active material is resistant to ribonuclease (RNase) and trypsin. After sensitive cells are incubated in antigen, the transfer factor is found in the supernatant, whereas the cells have become desensitized. It has also

been demonstrated that, in the case of delayed hypersensitivity to diphtheria toxoid, no antitoxin antibodies are demonstrable in the donor extracts or in recipients following transfer.

Dialysates of sensitive leukocyte extracts transfer delayed hypersensitivity. Fractionation of the dialysates of transfer factor on Sephadex G-25 suggests that the active substance has a molecular weight of less than 10,000. Such dialysates are also resistant to RNase.

Recently, transfer factor has been given to many patients with a variety of diseases associated with immunodeficiency (Wiskott-Aldrich syndrome, chronic mucocutaneous candidiasis, leprosy) and to patients with various malignancies, including melanoma and osteogenic sarcoma. A number of dramatic "cures" have been reported, but controlled clinical trials are necessary to determine the efficacy of transfer factor in these and other diseases.

Histopathology

The most striking feature of a delayed hypersensitivity lesion is an accumulation of mononuclear cells, especially around small blood vessels (Figure 51). In addition to lymphocytes, many macrophages and their lysosomal contents are revealed by electron microscopy or histochemical techniques. These macrophages originate from blood monocytes whose precursors are in the bone marrow. Lesions also show deposits of fibrin.

Polymorphonuclear leukocytes are seen in the infiltrates, but they are a minor component in delayed reactions in contrast to the Arthus reaction, in which they are the dominant cell type. Pathology ranges in severity from cellular infiltration to severe necrotic and fibrinoid vascular lesions to massive necrosis.

Origin of infiltrating cells: Experiments show that infiltrating cells are derived from the circulation – not from the skin itself. For example, one of a pair of identical twins was sensitized; skin grafts were then exchanged between the two. Subsequently, the skin test made on the sensitized skin, which had been transferred to the normal nonsensitized twin, was negative, but the skin test on the normal skin grafted onto the sensitized twin was positive. Autoradiographic studies of delayed hypersensitivity reactions in animals given ^{3}H-labeled thymidine before skin testing suggest that the infiltrating cells came from the bone marrow via the blood and that many of them had recently divided.

Mediation of tissue injury: The exact mechanism of tissue injury in delayed hypersensitivity reactions is unclear. Whereas complement activation plays a significant part in Arthus reactions and both gamma-globulin and complement are abundant in these lesions, these proteins have not been detected in dermal delayed hypersensitivity reactions. Recently, a patient with no detectable C3 showed a normal cutaneous-delayed hypersensitivity response. Vitamin A, which lyses lysosomes in vitro, suppresses delayed hypersensitivity in guinea pigs when given in large amounts. This suggests that the lysosomes, which contain many hydrolytic enzymes, may play some part in tissue destruction. Lysosomal enzymes may be released in lesions of delayed hypersensitivity by macrophages – cells known to contain abundant lysosomes.

In Vitro Studies on Cellular Hypersensitivity

Macrophage migration inhibition: To detect inhibition of macrophage migration, peritoneal exudate cells from sensitized guinea pigs are placed into capillary tubes, then allowed to migrate out of the tubes onto glass coverslips placed in culture chambers. The normal migration is inhibited when antigen to which the animal is sensitized is in the medium (Figure 52). The inhibition is easily quantitated and is immunologically specific. Furthermore, cells from animals making antibody, but not exhibiting delayed hypersensitivity, are not inhibited by antigen.

Cell types and migration-inhibitory factor: Two cell types predominate in peritoneal exudates. Seventy percent are macrophages; the remainder are mostly lymphocytes with a few polymorphonuclear leukocytes. Their involvement in the inhibition of macrophage migration may reflect the mechanisms that are operative in human delayed hypersensitivity (Figure 53).

The lymphocytes are the specifically sensitive cells in the exudate. If even one lymphocyte from a sensitized animal is among 99 macrophages from a normal animal, the entire population is inhibited from migrating when antigen is present in the medium. Apparently, lymphocytes react with antigen and produce a soluble material that curtails the migration of the normal macrophages.

Table 12
Some properties of guinea pig macrophage inhibitory factor

Properties	pH 3-MIF	pH 5-MIF
Isoelectric point	3.0 – 4.5	5.0 – 5.5
Apparent MW	65,000	25,000 – 40,000
Density determined by CsCl density gradient centrifugation	denser than albumin	same density as albumin
Susceptibility to a macrophage-associated proteinase	−	+
Susceptibility to trypsin	−	+
Susceptibility to neuraminidase	+	−
Susceptibility to chymotrypsin	+	+
Susceptibility to plasmin and thrombin	−	−
Heat stability at 56 C for 30 min	stable	stable

Macrophage inhibitory factor (MIF) is produced only by living lymphocytes; its production is blocked by puromycin, an inhibitor of protein synthesis. If peritoneal exudate cells from sensitized animals are freed of lymphocytes, the remaining cells (largely macrophages) are no longer inhibited from migrating by antigen. Thus, the sensitized lymphocytes mediate inhibition of migration but, when cultured alone, are not inhibited from migrating by antigen. Chemical and physical characterization of MIF using Sephadex fractionation, preparative electrophoresis, isoelectrofocusing, degradation by chymotrypsin and neuraminidase, and cesium chloride ultracentrifugation indicates that MIF from guinea pigs exists as two species. The first is a glycoprotein with a molecular weight of approximately 65,000; the second is a protein with a molecular weight of 25,000 to 40,000. The properties of guinea pig MIF are summarized in Table 12. Recent studies show that both human and mouse MIFs have many properties similar to guinea pig MIF.

Figure 52
Macrophage migration-inhibition test

	No antigen	Ovalbumin	Toxoid
Normal cells			
Ovalbumin – sensitive cells			
Toxoid – sensitive cells			

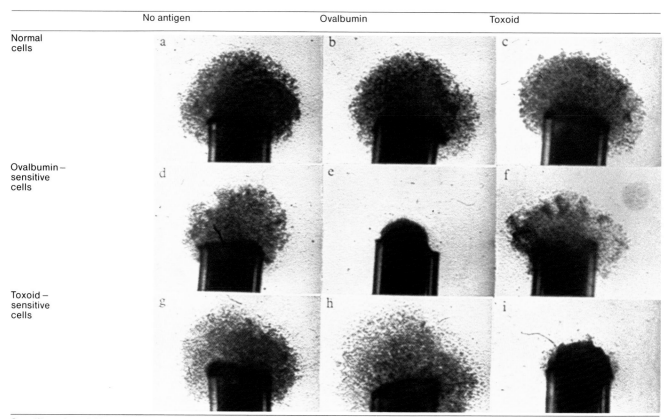

Specific antigen inhibits the normal migration of macrophages from capillary tubes.

Results from a number of experiments suggest that the macrophage receptor for MIF is a glycolipid-containing polymer composed of fucose and sialic acid residues. For instance, if guinea pig macrophages are incubated with fucosidase or neuraminidase (enzymes that remove fucose or sialic acid, respectively, from an oligosaccharide chain), macrophages no longer respond to the inhibitory factor. Further, when macrophages are incubated with an aqueous acidic glycolipid extracted from macrophages, they show an enhanced response to MIF. Glycolipids prepared from extracts of guinea pig neutrophils, guinea pig brain, or several other tissues do not enhance the response to MIF. Other types of cells also show greater responses to a hormone after the cells are first incubated with the glycolipid receptor for the hormone. Further, the macrophage glycolipid loses its enhancing activity if it is first treated with either fucosidase or neuraminidase. Analysis of the macrophage glycolipid suggests that it is a fucosylganglioside.

Other studies suggest that active proteases on the macrophage cell surface inhibit the effect of MIF. When macrophages are incubated with a number of different protease inhibitors, the MIF-induced inhibition of their migration is greatly enhanced. This can be explained, in part, by the recent finding that the activity of one species of MIF is destroyed by a macrophage-associated protease. This proteolysis may regulate the response of macrophages to the MIF.

Macrophage-activating factor: When macrophages are exposed to partially purified preparations of MIF, their behavior is altered in several ways (Table 13). Of special note, macrophages activated in vitro by lymphocyte mediators show enhanced microbicidal activity and enhanced cytotoxicity for neoplastic but not for normal cells. The lymphocyte mediator that alters or activates macrophages is called macrophage-activating factor (MAF) and seems to be indistinguishable from MIF. Recently, human MAF has been shown to activate human monocytes so that they also exhibit enhanced microbicidal and tumoricidal activity.

Figure 53
Pathways of delayed hypersensitivity lesions

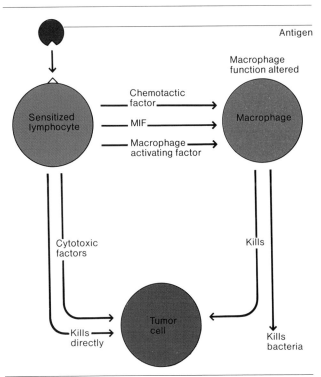

Not shown is the recent finding that usually macrophages are required to present the antigen to the sensitized lymphocyte.

**Table 13
Altered properties of macrophages induced
by lymphocyte mediators**

Increase in adherence to glass

Increase in ruffled membrane activity

Alteration in phagocytosis

Increase in membrane enzyme adenylate cyclase

Increase in glucose oxidation through hexose monophosphate shunt

Increase in uptake of glucosamine

Decrease in electron-dense surface material

Increase in pinocytosis

Increased Ca^{++} influx

Increase in number of cytoplasmic granules

Increase in cytoplasmic enzyme lactic dehydrogenase

Increased secretion of plasminogen activator

Increased complement (C2)

Increased prostaglandin production

Production of collagenase

Enhanced microbicidal activity

Enhanced tumoricidal activity

Chemotactic factor: When sensitized lymphocytes are incubated with specific antigen, they also produce a soluble factor that attracts macrophages. Thus, if macrophages are placed above a Millipore filter and supernatants from stimulated lymphocyte cultures are placed below the filter, the antigen-stimulated supernatants attract the macrophages through the filter. The chemotactic factor can be separated from MIF by electrophoresis on acrylamide gels and by cesium chloride ultracentrifugation. Unlike MIF, chemotactic factor is resistant to treatment with neuraminidase. Lymphocytes also make chemotactic factors for granulocytes.

Lymphocyte factors that regulate antibody responses: Soluble substances produced by lymphocytes are not restricted to participation in cell-mediated immunity. Indeed, lymphocyte mediators that are not immunoglobulins can profoundly affect the production of antibodies by lymphocytes – some enhance; others suppress. Some of these mediators act by affecting regulator T cells.

Other mediators: When stimulated by specific antigens, sensitized lymphocytes produce a number of soluble materials that have various biologic activities in addition to those described above. These are referred to as products of activated lymphocytes, or lymphokines (Table 14). To elucidate the biologic importance of these materials in vivo, they must be purified and characterized. Analysis of the roles of the various lymphocyte factors may help dissect the cellular hypersensitivity reaction in humans.

Postulated mechanisms in humans: These findings suggest a hypothetical mechanism for inciting the delayed hypersensitivity reaction in vivo. Antigen injected into the skin is presented on the macrophage to a few sensitized lymphocytes. These lymphocytes are stimulated to produce factors that increase vascular permeability and attract monocytes and macrophages to the site. The lymphocytes also produce MIF and MAF, both of which affect the behavior and function of macrophages once they are at the site. The macrophages may liberate lysosomal enzymes or other mediators, and they initiate a chain of events that leads to tissue damage or to the killing of microorganisms or tumor cells.

Clinical application: The in vitro assay for inhibition of migration has been adapted to study delayed hypersensitivity in humans. Blood lymphocytes stimulated by antigens in vitro synthesize an MIF-like factor that inhibits the migration of normal guinea pig macrophages or human monocytes but not polymorphonuclear leukocytes. This human MIF exists in two molecular species that resemble the factors found in the guinea pig. Another human mediator, leukocyte inhibitory factor (LIF), a protein with a molecular weight of 68,000, has been described; this inhibits the migration of polymorphonuclear leukocytes but not monocytes. LIF appears to be an esterase, because it is inhibited by esterase inhibitors such as diisopropyl fluorophosphate (DFP). The production of these and other mediators can help the physician assess certain lymphocyte functions in patients with immunodeficiency. Using these methods, it is also possible to study sensitivity to a variety of tissue antigens and drugs.

Clinical Aspects of Immunologic Deficiency Diseases

Diseases associated with immunologic deficiency can be categorized as those that involve either immunoglobulin or complement and those that reveal a deficiency of either cellular immunity or hypersensitivity. At times, several deficiencies occur in a single individual.

Although agammaglobulinemic patients with no other deficiency are especially susceptible to pyogenic infections, usually such patients can cope in a normal manner with viral and fungal infections. In contrast, patients with a cellular hypersensitivity deficiency are particularly prone to certain bacterial and protozoal infections caused by such organisms as *Mycobacterium tuberculosis*, *Pneumocystis carinii*, and *Pseudomonas aeruginosa*. Immune deficiency is also frequent in patients with progressive vaccinia (following vaccination with cowpox, Figure 54), disseminated herpes, and disseminated varicella. It is especially interesting that progressive vaccinia will occur in the presence of a high titer of circulating antibodies to the virus. Indeed, the occurrence of these infections in the presence of specific antibody, the complement system, and interferon emphasizes the important role of the cellular immune system in resistance to certain infections.

Table 14
Some lymphocyte mediators

I. Mediators affecting macrophages
a. Migration inhibitory factor (MIF)

b. Macrophage-activating factor (MAF) (indistinguishable from MIF)

c. Chemotactic factors for macrophages

d. Antigen-dependent MIF

II. Mediators affecting lymphocytes
a. Lymphocyte mitogenic factor (LMF)

b. Factors enhancing antibody formation (antigen specific and nonspecific)

c. Factors suppressing antibody formation or cell-mediated immunity (antigen specific and nonspecific)

III. Mediators affecting polymorphonuclear leukocytes
a. Chemotactic factors for neutrophils, eosinophils, and basophils

b. Leukocyte inhibitory factor (LIF)

c. Eosinophil-stimulation promoter

d. Histamine-releasing factor

IV. Mediators affecting other cells
a. Cytotoxic and growth inhibitory factors – lymphotoxin (LT)

b. Osteoclast-activating factor (OAF)

c. Collagen-producing factor

d. Colony-stimulating activity

e. Interferon

f. Skin-reactive factor

g. Immunoglobulin-binding factor

Figure 54
Child with delayed hypersensitivity deficiency who developed
generalized vaccinia

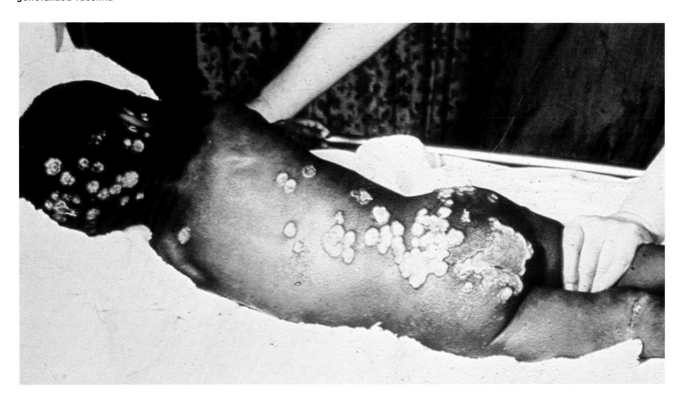

Some of the diseases associated with depressed cellular hypersensitivity are listed in Table 15 and will be described briefly below.

Severe combined immune deficiency: This severe immunologic deficiency occurs in male and female infants as an autosomal recessive trait; both cellular and humoral immune responses are lacking. Besides extreme thymic and lymphoid hypoplasia, the circulating lymphocyte count is low, and both antibody production and delayed hypersensitivity are lacking. Generally these infants contract pyogenic or viral infections shortly after birth and rarely survive beyond a year. There are some dramatic reports of immunologic reconstitution using bone marrow transplants from carefully matched donors, but thymus replacement failed to help these patients. Some of these patients lack the enzyme adenosine deaminase. This results in an accumulation of adenosine triphosphate, which is toxic to the cells that are the precursors of lymphocytes.

DiGeorge syndrome: In this condition, also known as congenital absence of thymus and parathyroids, the thymus is undeveloped, and the major deficiency is in the cellular immune system. Such patients can produce antibody, although it is not always quite normal. They have plasma cells and germinal centers in their lymph nodes, but in paracortical areas the lymphocytes are sparse to absent. X-ray examination shows that the thymus is absent and that circulating lymphocytes are very low. The patients also lack parathyroids and have low-serum calcium and tetany.

Patients with DiGeorge syndrome display no delayed hypersensitivity, cannot be actively sensitized with dinitrochlorobenzene (DNCB), and reject allografts poorly. Also, their lymphocytes do not respond to phyto-hemagglutinin (PHA) or antigens and do not make MIF in vitro. These patients frequently die of infections, although several instances of immunologic reconstitution after thymic transplantation have been reported.

Ataxia telangiectasia: This autosomal recessive disease occurs in children. It is characterized by neurologic abnormalities (especially progressive ataxia) as well as telangiectasis of the conjunctiva, face, and neck; there is also an increased incidence of gonadal dysgenesis and malignancy. Delayed hypersensitivity to natural antigens or to DNCB is low or absent. The patient cannot reject skin grafts promptly. The most frequent immunoglobulin defect is a depression of IgA.

Table 15
Conditions with impaired delayed hypersensitivity

Combined severe immunodeficiency

Congenital absence of thymus and parathyroids (DiGeorge syndrome)

Ataxis telangiectasia

Wiskott-Aldrich syndrome

Hodgkin disease and lymphosarcoma

Sarcoidosis

Lepromatous leprosy

Chronic mucocutaneous candidiasis

Secondary syphilis

Certain viral and parasitic diseases

Severe burns

Advanced malignancy

Malnutrition

Advanced rheumatoid arthritis

Systemic lupus erythematosus (?)

Pyoderma gangrenosum

Immunosuppressive therapy

Elderly with advanced diseases

Postoperative recovery period

Wiskott-Aldrich syndrome: This is a sex-linked disease associated with thrombocytopenia, eczema, and recurrent infections in young males. These boys respond abnormally to polysaccharide antigens, and their delayed hypersensitivity reactions are frequently impaired.

Hodgkin's disease: The primary immunologic defect in this disease is in delayed hypersensitivity, as manifested by decreased to absent reactions to natural antigens, frequent inability to be sensitized to antigens such as DNCB, and failure to reject skin grafts. Normal delayed hypersensitivity responses may often return during remissions.

Sarcoidosis: Delayed hypersensitivity is depressed in sarcoidosis, and it is more difficult to sensitize patients with this disease to DNCB than it is to sensitize normal persons.

Lepromatous leprosy: This disease causes depressed cellular hypersensitivity. Interestingly, in some patients, lymph-node paracortical areas are depleted of cells, and bacilli are prevalent. The number of T lymphocytes in the blood may be decreased.

Viral illnesses: It has long been known that delayed hypersensitivity is sometimes temporarily depressed during certain viral illnesses, especially measles and influenza. The mechanism of this depression is not known. Some studies suggest that the virus may have a direct effect on lymphocytes and may change their circulatory traffic pattern from blood to lymphoid organs.

Selected Bibliography

Cerottini JC, Brunner KT: Cell-mediated cytotoxicity, allograft rejection, and tumor immunity. *Adv Immunol 18*:67, 1974.

Cohen S, Pick E, Oppenheim J: *Biology of the Lymphokines.* New York, Academic Press, 1979, p 121.

David JR: Delayed hypersensitivity, in Brent L, Holborow J (eds): *Progress in Immunology II, Biological Aspects II.* Amsterdam, Elsevier North-Holland, 1974, vol 3, p 123-124.

David JR: Immunology, in Rubenstein E, Federman D (eds): *Scientific American Medicine,* ed 1. New York, Scientific American, 1979.

David JR, David RA: Cellular hypersensitivity and immunity: Inhibition of macrophage migration and lymphocyte mediators. *Prog Allergy 16*:300, 1972.

David JR, Remold HG: Macrophage activation by lymphocyte mediators and studies on the interaction of macrophage inhibitory factor (MIF) with its target cell, in Nelson DS (ed): *Immunobiology of the Macrophage.* New York, Academic Press Inc, 1976, p 401.

Doherty PC, Blanden RV, Zinkernagel RM: Specificity of virus-immune effector T cells for H-2K or H-2D compatible interactions: Implications for H-antigen diversity. *Transpl Rev 29*:89, 1976.

Remold HG, David JR: Cellular or delayed hypersensitivity, in Merscher PA, Muller-Eberhard HJ (eds): *Textbook of Immunopathology,* ed 2. New York, Grune & Stratton Inc, 1976, vol 1, p 157.

Transplantation Immunogenetics of HLA

6

Major Histocompatibility Complex

Embedded in the membrane of every human cell is an array of molecules (many of them glycoprotein) that are recognized by the immune system of another human as *antigens*. Normally, the body's immune system does not respond to its own membrane antigens because they are *self*. Transplanted foreign cells, however, carry *nonself* membrane antigens that can be recognized, and following this recognition, the cells carrying those antigens can be destroyed. Thus, for a successful transplant, there must be minimal differences between the antigens of the recipient and the donor, ie, the individuals must be histocompatible. Ultimately, of course, the search for compatibility requires an understanding of the genetic control of histocompatibility antigens.

A small segment of the chromosome is referred to as the major histocompatibility complex (MHC) and encodes within it the strongest histocompatibility, or transplantation, antigens. This complex of deoxyribonucleic acid (DNA) comprises approximately $\frac{1}{1000}$ of all the genetic material. These are the antigens that, if recognized as foreign on cells of an allograft, lead to rapid destruction of that allograft. Various aspects of the major histocompatibility complex in humans, referred to as HLA, are described in chapter 8.

Besides these very strong transplantation antigens, a number of other immunologically related phenomena are controlled by, or at least influenced by, genes located in the MHC, eg, immune responsiveness (Ir), susceptibility to some diseases, various components of the complement system, and cell-mediated responses against virally infected autologous or syngeneic cells. The evidence for Ir genes in humans is still fragmentary, although the MHC includes Ir genes in several other species (eg, mouse, guinea pig, rat, and rhesus monkey).

This chapter discusses the detection of histocompatibility antigens in humans and how they are controlled by MHC genes. Grafts may be rejected if incompatibilities exist for any one of a large number of other histocompatibility loci that are not encoded by the MHC (referred to as minor histocompatibility loci).

Figure 55
Schematic representation of HLA complex

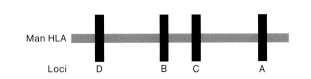

The vertical bars depict the four or five loci of HLA currently described whose alleles code for histocompatibility antigens. The HLA-A, -B and -C loci code for the classical serologically defined antigens that are present on essentially all cells of the body. In addition, these antigens are either the strongest targets for cytotoxic T lymphocytes or serve as excellent markers for those targets. The HLA-D locus codes for the LD antigens that stimulate the majority of proliferative responses in a primary MLC. It is thought that the serologically detected antigens that are related to HLA-D, the DR (D-related) antigens, may be encoded by a locus separate from HLA-D, but this point is not established.

Schematic Map of the HLA Complex

Figure 55 is a schematic of presently defined loci that code for histocompatibility antigens. By genetic convention, the centromere is always placed to the left of the diagram so that HLA-A is the furthest from the centromere. The HLA complex is located on chromosome C6.

For several years, only the HLA-A and -B loci were defined in the human MHC. The products of these loci, as discussed in more detail later, were detected by serological tests, and individuals were referred to as HLA-identical if they carried the same four antigens for these two loci. (Each individual can, of course, carry two different alleles for any one locus, one allele at each locus being inherited from each parent.) Later the HLA-C locus was detected and shown to produce a different cell, surface product from that produced by HLA-B. These three loci appear to code for products that serve the same function.

The HLA-D locus was first detected by using mixed leukocyte cultures, as will be discussed in detail below. There is evidence, however, that the HLA-D region is complex; several different determinants are encoded by a single HLA-D haplotype, and it is expected that there will be several loci within the D region. It is not yet established whether the D-related or DR antigens that can be detected by serological methods are encoded by a locus separate from HLA-D. One might expect that the HLA-D region is complex – by analogy with findings in mouse and guinea pig. In both of those species, the genetic region of the MHC that seems to be homologous with the HLA-D region in humans contains at least three different loci.

Markers for MHC Genes

Detection of antigens by serologic methods: The technique most commonly employed to detect cell-surface antigens with antisera is pictured in Figure 56. The antiserum, containing antibodies directed against a given histocompatibility antigen, is mixed with cells, incubated for a short time, and complement is added. If the cells carry the antigen against which the antibodies are directed, cell damage occurs in the presence of complement. By adding a vital dye, such as trypan blue or eosin, which is excluded from live cells but stains damaged cells, the number of damaged cells can be counted.

Using these serological methods, two types of antigens encoded by genes of the human MHC can be differentiated on the basis of their tissue distribution. One set of antigens, encoded by the HLA-A, -B, and -C loci (Table 16), is found on essentially all nucleated cells of the body. These are sometimes referred to as serologically defined (SD) antigens because they were the first HLA-encoded antigens that were detected by serological techniques. Antigens associated with another part of the MHC, called the HLA-D region, have a more limited tissue distribution and are found primarily on B lymphocytes, T lymphocytes, macrophages, epidermal cells, and sperm.

Figure 56
Complement-dependent, antibody-mediated lysis

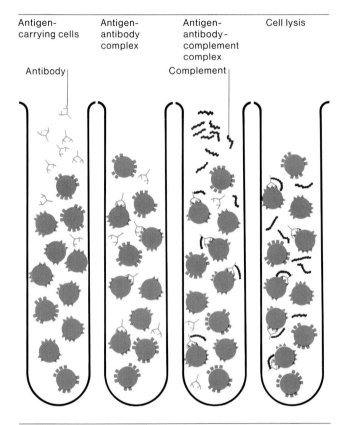

| Antigen-carrying cells | Antigen-antibody complex | Antigen-antibody-complement complex | Cell lysis |

Antibody / Complement

Antibody attaches to corresponding antigens on the cell membrane, and in the presence of complement, cells are lysed. This test is used to detect serologically defined histocompatibility antigens.

Table 16
Methods of detecting HLA antigens

Test procedures	HLA loci that encode antigens		
	D	B C A	
Serological methods	D-related (DR)	Classically serologically defined (SD)	
	(B cell, Ia-like)		
Cellular methods			
Mixed leukocyte culture	+	−	
Assay of cytotoxicity in CML	?	+	
Homozygous – typing cells	+	−	
Primed LD typing cells	+	−	

In humans, three SD loci are identified. The A, B, and C alleles determine the serologically defined (SD) antigens. In addition, there are serologically defined antigens known as DR antigens. Differences at the HLA-D locus lead to strong activation in MLC.

The serologically defined antigens of the HLA-D region are now referred to as the D-related (DR) antigens, to distinguish them from the SD antigens of HLA-A, -B, and -C. DR antigens are sometimes referred to as "Ia-like" or "B-cell" antigens because they were first found on B lymphocytes and are presumably comparable to the Ia antigens in the mouse. The serologically defined A, B, and C antigens and the D-region antigens not only have different tissue distributions but also have a different chemical structure and interact predominantly with different immune-cell populations.

Listed in Table 17 are the presently recognized antigens that are associated with the HLA complex. Poorly defined antigens carry a workshop (w) designation rather than the official World Health Organization (WHO) number.

Detection of antigens by cell-mediated immune responses: As an alternative to the use of antisera to detect cell-surface antigens, in vitro methods have been developed that use the response of T lymphocytes to measure the MHC-encoded antigens on the cell curface. The reason for using both serological and cellular approaches is that the antigenic determinants recognized by antibody and those recognized by T lymphocytes may not be identical.

The cellular assays attempt to recreate in vitro the responses of T lymphocytes when they encounter foreign antigens in vivo. The most commonly used test methods are the mixed leukocyte culture (MLC) and cell-mediated lympholysis (CML) assays, which are intimately related.

The MLC test has been used to detect not only alloantigens but also antigens on cells such as autologous leukemia cells. To match donor and recipient for transplantation (Figure 57), mononuclear cells from a potential organ donor's peripheral blood are first treated with x-irradiation or mitomycin C to prevent the cells from dividing and incorporating radioactive thymidine. These stimulating cells can still present their alloantigens on the cell surface. The stimulating cells are then mixed with a responding mononuclear cell population from the peripheral blood of a potential recipient. If the recipient cells, which are not treated with mitomycin C or x-irradiation, recognize the antigens on the donor cells as nonself (ie, foreign), they will begin to multiply and incorporate radioactive thymidine into their DNA.

Table 17
Antigens associated with HLA complex

Locus A	Locus B	Locus C	Locus D	Locus DR
A1	B5	Cw1	Dw1	DRw1
A2	B7	Cw2	Dw2	DRw2
A3	B8	Cw3	Dw3	DRw3
A9	B12	Cw4	Dw4	DRw4
A10	B13	Cw5	Dw5	DRw5
A11	B14	Cw6	Dw6	DRw6
A25(10)	B15		Dw7	DRw7
A26(10)	B17		Dw8	
A28	B18		Dw9	
A29	B27		Dw10	
Aw19	B37		Dw11	
Aw23(9)	B40			
Aw24(9)	Bw4			
Aw30	Bw6			
Aw31	Bw16			
Aw32	Bw21			
Aw33	Bw22			
Aw34	Bw35			
Aw36	Bw38(16)			
Aw43	Bw39(16)			
	Bw41			
	Bw42			
	Bw44(12)			
	Bw45(12)			
	Bw46			
	Bw47			
	Bw48			
	Bw49(21)			
	Bw50(21)			
	Bw51(5)			
	Bw52(5)			
	Bw53			
	Bw54(22)			

In an MLC test, at least two different subpopulations of recipient lymphocytes respond by proliferating. The response of each population can be primarily related to either the ABC region or the D region. First, the helper T lymphocytes of the recipient respond to HLA-D antigens; the determinants recognized by the helper T lymphocyte are referred to as LD (L determinants or lymphocyte defined). This response constitutes the majority of the cell division seen in an MLC, although it is not established what percentage of the dividing cells are helper cells. In fact, it was this proliferative response in an MLC that was first used to define the HLA-D locus. Second, precursor cytotoxic T lymphocytes respond to antigens associated with HLA-A, -B, and -C loci. We refer to the target antigens that are recognized by these cytotoxic T lymphocytes as CD (C determinants or cytotoxicity-defined). The recognition of CD by cytotoxic T lymphocytes will be discussed later in this chapter.

Because division of the helper T lymphocytes predominates in an MLC, the overall thymidine incorporation is frequently used as a measure of the amount of HLA-D region (LD) disparity between the donor and recipient cells tested. Of course, if the donor and recipient have identical HLA-D regions, there is little or no proliferative response. The results of an MLC test, therefore, indicate whether the donor and recipient have the same HLA-D region or the degree of HLA-D disparity.

Antigens of the D Region
As already suggested, serological methods and cellular tests, such as the mixed leukocyte culture and cell-mediated lympholysis assays, may well detect different determinants on the cell surface. For instance, it has been suggested that there are separate loci in the HLA-D region that code for the DR determinants recognized serologically and the LD antigens recognized in the mixed leukocyte culture; it is equally possible that DR and LD are different determinants on the same molecule. In addition to serological methods, two new procedures have been developed to define, by cellular methods, determinants encoded by the HLA region. These two methods are the homozygous typing cell and primed LD typing tests.

Figure 57
Mixed lymphocyte culture

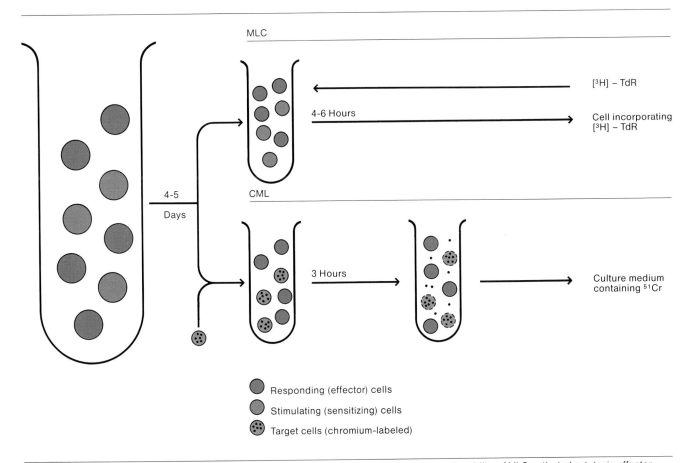

MLC

[³H] – TdR

4-6 Hours

Cell incorporating [³H] – TdR

4-5
Days

CML

3 Hours

Culture medium containing ⁵¹Cr

Responding (effector) cells

Stimulating (sensitizing) cells

Target cells (chromium-labeled)

The MLC measures the proliferation of responding lymphocytes to foreign antigens presented by stimulating cells. Proliferation is measured by assaying the amount of tritiated thymidine (³H-TdR) incorporated into the DNA of responding cells that divide during a four to five day culture period. To prevent stimulating cells from incorporating ³H-TdR, they are irradiated before adding to the responding cells.

The CML measures the ability of MLC-activated cytotoxic effector cells to lyse chromium-labeled (⁵¹Cr) target cells that carry the same antigens as the original stimulating cells. Lysis is measured by the ⁵¹Cr released from the specific lysed target cells.

See text for the discussion of the nature of the antigens that activate MLC and CML responses and of the cell types activated by these antigens.

Homozygous typing cells (HTCs): Suppose we have lymphocytes from an individual who is homozygous for the HLA-D locus and carries the antigen Dw1. If we use this cell, called a homozygous typing cell (HTC), as the stimulating cell in an MLC, responding cells that lack the Dw1 antigen will show a strong proliferative response to the HTC because they recognize Dw1 as foreign. However, the responding cells will show a very weak response, or none at all, if they carry the Dw1 antigen. To determine whether the responding cell carries other D-locus antigens, HTCs of other Dw specificities can be used in a similar manner.

Homozygous typing cells have now been obtained for 11 different D-region antigens and are referred to as Dw1, Dw2 . . . Dw11. The D-region antigens also appear to be complex; Dw clusters may overlap and code for a shared determinant while each also codes for determinants not specified by the other cluster. D-region antigens as measured with HTCs are frequently referred to as "clusters," since it is thought that one D haplotype may code for several different determinants. For instance, what we refer to as Dw6 may represent several different determinants present on one or more molecules.

Primed LD typing (PLT): An alternative and more rapid approach for defining HLA-D region antigens involves *sensitizing* or *educating* responding lymphocytes in vitro and using their immunological memory to speed recognition of LD antigens (Figure 58). Responding cells of one individual (A) are mixed with mitomycin C-treated or x-irradiated stimulating cells taken from a second individual (B), where individuals A and B differ only for a single HLA-D haplotype. After culturing for ten days, most of the cells in the MLC have

Figure 58
The primed LD typing test

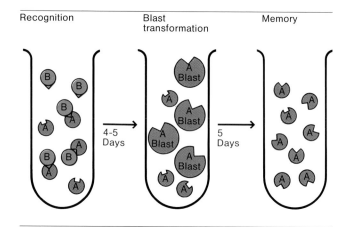

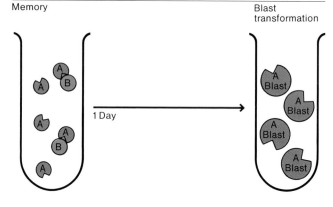

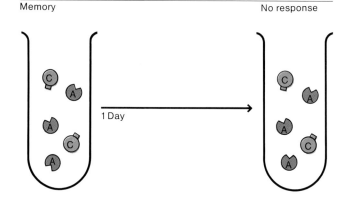

Responding cells of individual A that recognize foreign antigen(s) on the cells of individual B divide, transform into blast cells, and then revert to small memory lymphocytes. If such memory cells are now reexposed to the sensitizing antigen on the cells of individual B, or any other individual carrying that antigen, they will very rapidly divide and transform into blast cells. This reaction can be measured by studying the incorporation of radioactive thymidine. If such memory cells are not confronted with the specific antigen to which they were sensitized, no response takes place.

stopped dividing. If these primed LD typing (PLT) cells from individual A are restimulated on day ten with cells from B, the memory T cells of donor A rapidly proliferate. The proliferation can be quantitated by measuring radioactive thymidine incorporation that occurs within 24 hours after restimulation. Of course, any other cell that shares the same HLA-D region (LD) antigens to which A was sensitized in the original ten-day MLC test will restimulate a similar rapid proliferative response. Conversely, cells that do not carry the particular antigens recognized by that PLT cell will not restimulate a strong, secondary-type, rapid proliferative response. Thus, a series of different PLT cells, each educated to recognize a different antigen, can be used to type the LD antigens on the cells of any one individual. Various laboratories now have many different PLT cells that recognize between seven and ten antigens (PL1, PL2, etc). The exact relationship between the LD antigens defined by homozygous typing cells and the antigens defined with primed LD typing cells is not known.

CD Antigens of the HLA-A, -B, -C Regions

Cytotoxic T lymphocytes generated in an MLC recognize antigenic determinants associated with the HLA-A, -B, and -C loci. However, in all cases, the determinants encoded by these loci, which are recognized serologically, may not be identical to those recognized by the cytotoxic T lymphocytes. For instance, target cells bearing certain HLA-A, -B, or -C antigens will be lysed by cytotoxic T lymphocytes sensitized to stimulating cells with the same HLA-A, -B, and -C serologically defined antigens. Occasionally, however, such sensitized cytotoxic T-lymphocyte cells will show aberrant reactions, ie, the cytotoxic cells will lyse target cells carrying none of the serologically defined HLA-A, -B, and -C antigens "recognized" as foreign in the initial sensitizing MLC. Such cytotoxic T-lymphocyte preparations presumably recognize cytotoxicity-defined (CD) antigens that are different from SD antigens.

So far, three CD determinants have been defined that do not correlate with any of the known serologically defined antigens. To what extent the separate definition of CD will be useful in typing unrelated individuals must still be determined.

Relationship of Serologically and Cellularly Defined Determinants

It is still unclear whether antigens in the D region that are recognized by antibodies are identical with determinants in the D region that are recognized using the cellular techniques (MLC or PLT). Nor is it clear whether the HLA-A, -B, and -C determinants, which were found using serological methods (SD), are identical with those defined by cytotoxic T lymphocytes (CD). The question of identity of determinants encoded by either the same gene or very closely linked genes is important. Even if the determinants recognized serologically and those recognized by cellular techniques are different, the two types of determinants may be carried by the same molecule, ie, encoded by the same gene (see Figure 59).

LD-CD collaboration and the development of CML: The majority of proliferating lymphocytes in an MLC respond to the LD determinants encoded in the HLA-D region, whereas the cytotoxic T lymphocytes respond to the CD determinants associated with HLA-A, -B, and -C loci. Thus, two separate T-lymphocyte subpopulations that serve different functions respond to LD and CD respectively. T cells that, by themselves, cannot mediate cytotoxicity and presumably cannot alone cause allograft rejection respond to LD and are called helper T cells. To enhance the development of the cytotoxic response, helper T cells cooperate with cytotoxic T lymphocytes that have responded to foreign CD determinants.

Figure 59
Possible relationship of SD and CD antigens

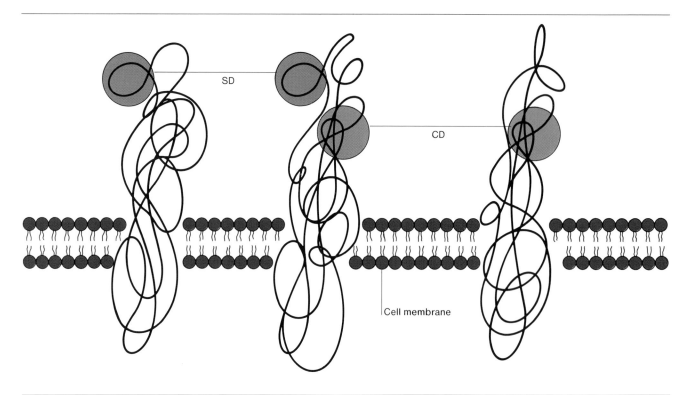

Alternate models to illustrate how determinants of the HLA-A, -B, and -C loci are recognized by antibodies or cytotoxic lymphocytes. Center: A single gene product exists, and different parts of the molecule are recognized by either antibody or by cytotoxic L lympho-cyte. The two sites need not be totally different and can overlap. Two separate gene products exist, one recognized by the antibody (left molecule), the other by the cytotoxic T lymphocyte (right molecule).

A precursor cytotoxic T lymphocyte is primed to recognize CD antigens on the stimulating cell in the MLC (Figure 60). This recognition, called signal 1, is believed to induce precursor differentiation to a "poised" state in which the cytotoxic T lymphocyte is receptive to help. *Help* is either a soluble factor, presumably released from LD-activated T helper cells, or is conveyed by direct contact between the cytotoxic and helper T cells. We refer to the interaction of the helper factor with the developing cytotoxic T lymphocyte as *signal 2*. Presumably, the combination of signals 1 and 2 leads to the maximal cytotoxic response (see chapter 6).

In addition to the cytotoxic T lymphocyte and the helper T lymphocyte, a third functionally disparate subpopulation of T lymphocytes exists, called the T-suppressor cells. The suppressor T lymphocytes can also be activated by alloantigens encoded by MHC genes. In the development of a cytotoxic response, the suppressor T lymphocytes play a balancing, homeostatic role with the helper cell.

Role of MHC Antigens in Allograft Rejection

If a kidney is transplanted between two siblings who have inherited the same HLA haplotypes from their parents and have identical HLA antigens, then, in more than 90% of cases, grafts survive for many years. In fact, when graft survival exceeds two years, there is little reason to believe that the kidney will be rejected. However, in seeking donors for nonsibling graft recipients, the problem confronting the immunogeneticist and clinician is to determine which of the antigens within HLA is of greatest importance in determining graft survival. To date, most studies have matched donor and recipient for the HLA-A and -B SD antigens because few antisera were available for the HLA-C locus antigens; such matching has little salutary effect in promoting graft survival.

Several groups have attempted to match the HLA-D LD antigens between donor and recipient. Most of these studies have involved either prospective mixed leukocyte culture tests using donor cells from living relatives or retrospective tests using cadaver donors. The data strongly suggest that compatibility for HLA-D, ie, minimizing the amount of MLC disparity as measured by tritiated thymidine incorporation, is related to improved graft survival.

Figure 60
Collaboration of helper and cytotoxic lymphocytes

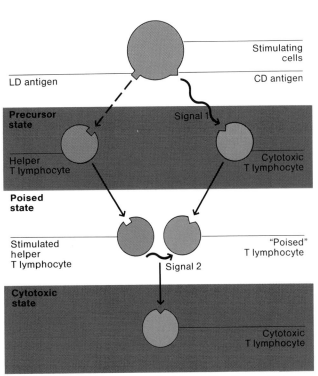

The response of T lymphocytes to the LD and CD antigens of the stimulating cells leads to a maximum cytotoxic effect. It is not clear whether the suppressor T lymphocyte recognizes the same CD determinant that is also recognized by the cytotoxic T lymphocyte.

More recently, studies have been done using serological reagents against the HLA-DR antigens. Such serological studies attempt to correlate the disparity for HLA-DR antigens with graft survival and yield data that are consistent with results obtained using mixed leukocyte cultures. That is, if donor and recipient share one DR haplotype and differ in only the second, graft survival is better than in donor-recipient combinations whose cells differ for both DR haplotypes. Similarly, graft survival is improved if donor and recipient share both DR haplotypes.

At least two mechanisms might explain why D-region matching improves graft survival. First, as already discussed, the response of helper T lymphocytes to LD antigens increases the level of cytotoxicity that is generated in vitro. If similar cellular reactions take place in vivo, the absence of foreign LD antigens decreases the magnitude of the cytotoxic T- lymphocyte response and improves chances of graft survival. This mechanism would probably be favored by most transplantation immunologists in view of the very strong role that T lymphocytes presumably play in allograft rejection. Second, helper T lymphocytes also function in T- and B-cell collaboration (chapter 4). Because antibody secreted by B lymphocytes is important in graft rejection, a decrease in T-cell help to B lymphocytes would reduce the strength of the antibody response against the graft.

Relative strength of antigens: In addition to counting the *number* of antigens that differ between the donor and recipient, the immunogenic *strength* of the various antigens should be measured. Using the mixed-leukocyte culture test, we obtain a measure of the strength of LD incompatibility between donor and recipient. When we serologically define the specific antigens of the major histocompatibility complex loci, we know only that a given donor and recipient differ in, for example, two antigens. However, we cannot state how strong the cellular response will be to the two antigens.

Recently introduced tests measure the degree of LD and CD incompatibility between donor and recipient. Their clinical usefulness will be evaluated in the next several years.

Summary: In matching donor and recipient for transplantation, we are faced with a dilemma. Although the HLA complex is preeminent in determining the fate of an allograft, it is not clear which determinants or combinations of determinants must be matched if maximal graft survival is to be obtained. It appears that matching for the LD antigens of the donor and recipient (using the mixed-leukocyte culture) or matching for the DR antigens will improve the results of transplantation. Because several days are required to perform MLC tests, they are not useful for prospective matching in cadaver transplantation. Perhaps the more recently described primed LD-typing tests will allow more expedient matching before cadaver transplantation.

Role of Major Histocompatibility Complex Antigens in "Reactions to Syngeneic or Autologous Abnormal Cells"

An exciting area in immunology concerns the role that MHC antigens play in the immune response to autologous (or syngeneic) transformed or virus-infected cells. If lymphocytes from a mouse are sensitized to virus-infected autologous or syngeneic cells, then a cytotoxic reaction develops against newly expressed antigens on the virus-infected cells. If these newly expressed antigens were simply those associated with viral infection, it might be expected that cells of a mouse that is sensitized to syngeneic virus-infected cells would also lyse target cells of an allogeneic mouse infected with the same virus. This, however, is not the case. In most instances, there is a *dual requirement* for lysis of the target cells (Table 18). First, the target cells must be infected with the same virus used to infect the syngeneic sensitizing cells. Second, the target cells must carry the same MHC cytotoxicity-defined (CD) determinants present on the responding and the sensitizing cells. Of course, the responding and sensitizing cells carry the same MHC CD antigens because they are from either the same individual (autologous) or same strain (syngeneic). Thus, the cytotoxic T lymphocytes that are sensitized to the newly expressed antigens on the virally transformed cells appear to recognize both the viral product and the MHC CD determinants.

Table 18
Reactions of cytotoxic T lymphocytes to cells of various strains infected with the same virus

Sensitizing MLC		Target cells infected with virus			
Responding cell	Sensitizing (stimulating) cells	Strain	H-2K antigen	H-2D antigen	CML
strain A normal	strain A virus infected	A	K^a	D^a	+++
		B	K^a	D^x	++
		C	K^b	D^b	–

If the responding cells of strain A are sensitized to the virus-infected cells of the same strain, then the resulting cytotoxic T lymphocytes will efficiently kill virus infected target cells only if they carry the CD determinants of that strain. (In mice, the H-2K and H-2D CD antigens are analogous and probably homologous with the human HLA-A, -B, and -C locus associated CD antigens.) Thus, as illustrated, if strain A has been sensitized to the virus-infected cells of strain A, then virus-infected target cells of strain A will be lysed. Target cells of strain B infected with the same virus and sharing the same CD antigens of the H-2K locus (K^a) will also be lysed but less efficiently, presumably because they share the K locus-associated CD determinants. Strain C target cells (K^b and D^b) that share neither K^a nor D^a locus CD determinants with the sensitizing strain are not lysed significantly even though infected with the same virus.

Two explanations have been offered for these findings. First, the viral protein expressed on the cell surface may complex with the MHC CD antigen of, for example, the strain A cell. Thus, a new antigenic determinant is formed by this molecular interaction that is specific for the complex between the CD antigen(s) of strain A and the viral protein. Now, if the same viral protein complexes with different MHC CD antigen(s) of strain B, a different new antigenic determinant would be formed. This new antigen would not be recognized by cytotoxic T lymphocytes sensitized to the complex of the viral product with the MHC antigen of strain A. Second, it has been suggested that cytotoxic T lymphocytes can simultaneously recognize both the viral product and the MHC CD antigen on the target cell. This concept of *dual recognition* is also consistent with the finding that only those target cells that carry both the particular virus and the same H-2 CD antigen would be lysed. In addition, the cytotoxic response against minor histocompatibility loci (ie, not in the MHC) may also be expressed only when the sensitizing cell and the target cell share those minor antigens and the CD antigens coded in the MHC of the sensitizing cell.

Overview of the MHC

Control of many different phenomena that are directly or indirectly related to immunological function has been ascribed to genes of the major histocompatibility complex. The block of genetic information that codes for these traits has been held together in evolution for a very long time. It would appear most likely that, at least in part, the MHC evolved to survey for altered-self, eg, new antigens appearing on, for instance, virus-infected cells. This is an attractive hypothesis, but we must also consider that the MHC includes genes as varied as those controlling immune response and those influencing mating behavior. Clearly, much has to be learned about the broader role of the MHC. At the very least, our increased understanding of the various antigens of the MHC and of allograft rejection will markedly improve the results of clinical transplantation.

Suggested Reading

Bach FH, van Rood JJ: The major histocompatibility complex – genetics and biology. N Engl J Med 295:806-813, 872-878, and 927-936, 1976.

Glossary

Allele. Any of several forms of one gene, usually arising through mutation, that are responsible for hereditary variation.

Allograft. A graft of tissue or an organ between two genetically dissimilar individuals of the same species.

Autologous. Refers to cells or tissue from one individual.

CD — C determinants or cytotoxicity-defined. These determinants, encoded by major histocompatibility complex (MHC) genes, are target antigens for cytotoxic T lymphocytes.

CML — Cell-mediated lympholysis. This assay measures cytotoxic T lymphocytes that lyse target cells carrying either the sensitizing antigens previously encountered (eg, in mixed leukocyte culture, MLC) or antigens that cross-react with the sensitizing antigens.

Haplotype. The MHC genes or other genes on *one* chromosome. Each individual has two haplotypes, one inherited from the father, one inherited from the mother, that together comprise the individual's genotype.

HTCs – Homozygous typing cells. These are cells that are homozygous for the HLA-D region. HTCs can be used as stimulating cells in a primary MLC to "type" the donor of the responding cells; if the HLA-D antigens of the responder fail to proliferate (or proliferate relatively weakly), they have the same, or similar, HLA-D antigens as the HTCs.

LD – L Determinants or lymphocyte-defined. These antigenic structures or determinants stimulate a proliferative response in a primary mixed-leukocyte culture. Some of the cells that proliferate are presumed to be helper T lymphocytes. The LD determinants are primarily encoded by the HLA-D region in humans and the H-2 I region in mice.

Locus. The chromosomal position of a gene as determined by its linear order relative to the other genes on that chromosome.

MHC – Major histocompatibility complex. This chromosomal segment (HLA in humans, H-2 in mice) encodes the strongest transplantation antigens. Genes of the MHC, or closely associated genes, are involved in disease susceptibility, immune response, and synthesis of certain components of the complement pathway.

MLC – Mixed leukocyte culture. Lymphocytes from two individuals are mixed in vitro. The stimulating cells of one individual are usually treated with mitomycin-C or x-irradiation to prevent division, although they can still present their antigens to the second population, ie, the responding lymphocytes. If the latter cells divide, LD disparity between the individuals is indicated.

PLT – Primed LD typing. This method is used to define HLA-D region determinants (and perhaps others encoded by genes outside the HLA-D region). Lymphocytes are primed in a mixed-leukocyte culture, then allowed to revert to "memory" lymphocytes; the latter used as responding cells in a secondary mixed-leukocyte culture.

SD – Serologically defined. These determinants are recognized by antibodies in standard histocompatibility typing tests. They are encoded by HLA-A, -B, and -C genes in humans. HLA-D may also have serologically detectable antigens, referred to as DR (D-related), as well as the LD determinants.

Syngeneic. Refers to cells or tissue from the same inbred strain, eg, two animals that are, at least as a first approximation, genetically identical.

7

Transplantation Immunology

Histocompatibility and Inheritance

The concept of regulation of tissue transplantability or histocompatibility arose from the experimental use of inbred strains of mice that became genetically identical after several generations of brother-sister mating and selection. Skin transplantation within an inbred line is successful when a syngeneic graft is used (isograft, using old terminology), whereas allogeneic grafts (allografts) carried out between different lines are rejected (homografts, using old terminology). Mating mice of two different inbred lines yields an F_1 hybrid that accepts tissue from either parental strain; however, the parental strains will reject the hybrid grafts.

These *genetic laws of transplantation* ultimately led to development of a co-dominant genetic theory for the transmission of the *transplantability* determinants (Figure 61). The F_1 hybrid does not recognize tissue from either parent as different from itself. Conversely, either parent recognizes tissue from the F_1 hybrid as different, because of antigens the offspring inherited from the other parent, and rejects the tissue.

The percentage of backcross (parent $\times$ F_1 hybrid) and F_2 hybrid (F_1 hybrid $\times$ F_1 hybrid) animals that accept tissues from the parental strains depends upon the number of Mendelian-dominant genes controlling graft rejection. These breeding experiments suggest that as many as 30 or more different, independently segregating genetic loci determine transplantability.

Histocompatibility loci are chromosomal regions where histocompatibility genes reside. These sites are occupied by the multiple alleles (one is present on each of the paired chromosomes) that ultimately determine the specificities of the cell membrane "transplantation antigens."

Not all transplantation antigens stimulate the host's immune reactions equally. Genes determining transplant antigens that elicit a mild allograft reaction are called *weak*. Other loci code for transplant antigens that evoke vigorous rejection are termed *strong*. The major histocompatibility complex (MHC) codes for "strong" allograft immunity. Histocompatibility antigens may also evoke an additive response. For example, if a graft differs from its host at multiple weak loci, it may be vigorously rejected.

In humans, the strong histocompatibility antigens are encoded by a complex genetic region called the major histocompatibility complex (MHC), which is located on the short arm of the 6th chromosome. This region, known as HLA (human leukocyte antigen),

Figure 61
Transmission of the determinants of transplantability

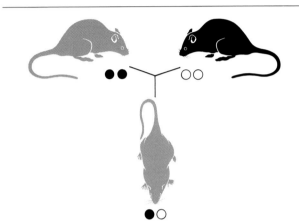

Mating homozygous inbred strains ●● and ○○ gives the heterozygous F_1 ●○ hybrid.

F_1 ●○ hybrid accepts parental ●● skin graft.

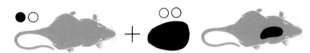

F_1 ●○ hybrid accepts parental ○○ skin graft.

Parental ●● strain rejects F_1 ●○ hybrid skin graft.

Parental ○○ strain rejects F_1 ●○ hybrid skin graft.

Skin-graft rejection depends on donor possessing an antigen absent in the recipient.

codes for HLA antigens that are involved in basic biologic processes (see chapters 4, 6, and 8) and in evoking strong allograft immunity. The characterization of transplantation antigens is the basis for most tissue-typing tests performed before an organ allograft. This complex genetic region is further subdivided into four loci (A, B, C, and D), each bearing genes that determine cell-surface HLA. The A, B, and C locus genes code for antigens that are serologically detectable (SD) and are found on the surface of all nucleated cells including T and B lymphocytes and macrophages. They are also known as classical type I antigens.

These type I antigens bind cytotoxic antibody, which destroys allografts during humoral rejection, and is used with complement in tissue-typing reactions. The antigens determined by the A and B loci evoke strong immunity, whereas C-locus antigens evoke weak immunity. The D region determines cell-surface antigens found on B lymphocytes, monocytes, a small subpopulation of T lymphocytes, and both epidermal and endothelial cells. The latter antigens are thought to be associated with immune responsiveness. Because B lymphocytes and macrophages are stimulators in the mixed lymphocyte-culture reaction, the antigens determined by the D region are called lymphocyte-defined, or LD, antigens. When B-lymphocyte alloantigens are detected by serologic means, they are called DR antigens. (The D and DR designations are discussed in chapter 6.) These antigens are also known as type II.

Another rather important histocompatibility system in humans is the ABH (ABO) blood classification system for determining red-blood-cell antigens. These cell-surface antigens are also transplantation antigens, and the rules governing transfusion matching apply. The Lewis blood-group antigen is thought to function as a histocompatibility antigen under some conditions, because renal allografts are more likely to fail in Le^{a-b-} (negative) recipients when the donor is Le^{a+b+}. Because the negative genotype is rare, this problem is not common.

Role of Transplantation Antigens

Transplantation antigens are a structural part of the cell membrane and are detected by numerous well-characterized immunologic reactions (Figure 62). Histocompatibility antigens can be extracted from most body tissues, the highest content being in tissues of lymphoid or hematopoietic origin.

Theoretically, each nucleated cell in the body may carry transplantation antigens on its surface. However, differentiated cell types may vary considerably, both in the amount of antigen present and the immunogenicity expressed. This variability depends on the relative lack of antigen, the spatial configuration of the antigen, and the localization of the antigen, which make it difficult for the immune system to recognize. For example, in whole organ grafts such as kidney, many cells with membrane-associated antigenic specificity may be sheltered from the immunologically competent cell by tissue basement membranes. Such protection is not afforded heart tissue, thus the parenchymal cell is more vulnerable to damage.

Some transplantation antigens may occur in soluble form; however, their function is unknown. Following solubilization, antigenic activity is found in the lipoprotein fraction associated with the plasma membranes of lymphocytes. Further hydrolysis of the lipoprotein yields glycopeptides that retain antigenic specificity. The amino acid sequence of some human histocompatibility antigens has been determined. Not only does this chemical characterization permit comparison between surface antigens but it may also improve methods for inducing immunologic tolerance and enhancement and for producing tissue-typing reagents.

Tissue Typing

Presently, serologic and biologic methods are used in tissue typing and in genetic donor-recipient matching before organ transplantation. The serologic tests identify specific transplantation antigens, and the matching of donor and recipient depends on the number of shared antigens. For each of the loci of the MHC, from zero to two antigens will match. The biologic tests measure the strength of expression of genetic differences by using the in vitro mixed lymphocyte culture (MLC) reaction. (The theoretical approach to typing is outlined in chapter 6.)

Figure 62
Localization of a surface transplantation antigen

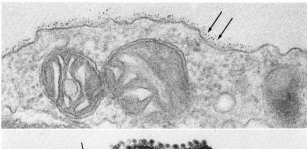

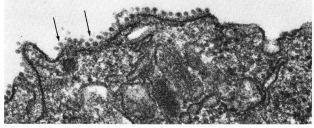

Localization of a surface transplantation antigen (histocompatibility-2b) on a mouse lymph node lymphocyte used either ferritin (top) or southern bean mosaic virus (SBMV) (bottom) as the visual marker. Cell was first exposed to the specific transplant antibody synthesized in another mouse strain, then exposed to a hybrid antibody rabbit antimouse IgG/rabbit antiferritin (or anti-SBMV) and finally exposed to ferritin or SBMV. Thus, there are three layers of reactants necessary to visualize the location of the antigen. The hybrid antibody is the intermediate that links specific antibody to the marker.

Serologic typing: The lymphocytotoxicity test is the most widely used method of typing antigens that are found on leukocyte membranes (Figure 63). Lymphocytes are treated with complement and a series of standardized antisera. Cell damage is determined by (1) phase microscopy, (2) staining with vital dyes (eosin or trypan blue are taken up by dead cells), (3) enzymatic hydrolysis of fluorescein diacetate (viable cells fluoresce), and (4) prelabeling lymphocytes with ^{51}Cr (dying cells release of ^{51}Cr). These techniques are applied to both T- and B-lymphocyte typing for the A-, B-, C-, and D-region antigens.

Another important serologic test used prior to organ transplantation is the cross-match test, which detects preformed antibody in the serum of the recipient toward donor alloantigens. The prefix *allo* indicates that these antigens are detected within and are characteristic of a species. In the presence of such antibody against donor tissue, the organ allograft will almost always undergo a very rapid and generally irreversible process called *hyperacute rejection*. The recipient makes alloantibodies because of previous transfusions (whole blood, plasma, or plasma products), pregnancy, previous graft rejection, or preimmunization with microbial antigens that have some cross-reactivity with the transplant alloantigens. In addition, before transplantation, this antibody test can screen the reactivity of a patient's serum antibodies to lymphocytes from random cell donors. If a patient's serum reacts with 50% or more of random lymphocytes, there is a reduced chance for a successful allograft. The cross-matching does not detect *blocking* or *enhancing* antibody which, in some pretransplant patients, reacts with B lymphocytes at 4 C and is associated with improved graft survival. Presumably, these "cold antibodies" are specific for the D region, immunoglobulin, or another antigenic system of B lymphocytes.

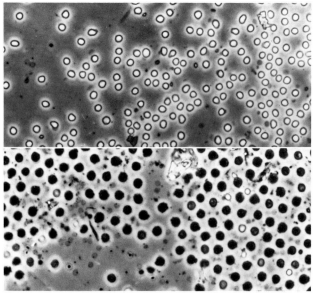

The lymphocytotoxicity test findings are normal if cells remain viable (top), abnormal if 20% or more are dead (bottom).

Biologic typing: When lymphocytes from two individuals are mixed together in short-term tissue cultures, T lymphocytes are transformed into large immature blast cells. This mixed leukocyte culture (MLC) reaction is a function of immunogenetic disparity or antigenic incompatibility between the D region type II antigens of the major histocompatibility complex of unsensitized individuals.

The measurement of cell division in MLC requires three to seven days, depending on the method used. Generally, the degree of cell division is measured by incorporation of radioisotopes into new DNA, RNA, or protein. Of course, if both donor and recipient lymphocytes react against each other, a measurement of DNA synthesis reflects the activity of both populations. To eliminate the contribution of lymphocytes from one of the two individuals, the donor cells are pretreated with mitomycin or x-irradiation to stop DNA synthesis. This test determines D-locus identity within families as well as unrelated donors and also indicates the general degree of proliferative response of a particular donor-recipient pair.

The cell-mediated lympholysis (CML) test uses sensitized lymphocytes that react with target cells (see chapter 6). The MLC reaction depends on recognition of antigens of the D locus, whereas the CML test depends on the recognition of serologically detectable antigens. The MLC and CML reactions are functions of different subsets of the T-lymphocyte population. The CML test may be an in vitro measure of the effector arc of allograft immunity, which results in parenchymal cell death. Indeed, during severe rejection of renal allografts, cytotoxic T lymphocytes are present in the circulation and in the inflammatory infiltrates of the allograft.

Certain antisera can block both the MLC and the CML test. Blocking activity can be found in a patient's serum both before and after transplantation; its biologic role is still unclear. Killer (K) cells can also kill target cells in vitro, even in the absence of complement, when they bind the Fc portion of the immunoglobulin (lymphocyte-dependent antibody, or LDA) that is attached to the target. This phenomenon is also referred to as antibody-dependent cellular cytotoxicity (ADCC).

After rejection of an allograft, inhibition of leukocyte migration detects cell-mediated immunity to HLA antigens in general – not just to the type I antigens.

From a clinical standpoint, tissue typing and matching are critically important for living and nonliving donor allografts. Transplants from matched siblings have an excellent posttransplant prognosis; one of four siblings will be HLA-identical and MLC nonreactive. Haplotype identical (half chromosomal identity) donors, either parental or sibling, are also suitable. Regardless of whether donors are living and related or are nonliving, a negative crossmatch test, indicating the absence of preformed lymphocytotoxic antibody, is essential to avoid hyperacute rejection.

Heart transplantation requires nonliving donor matching comparable to that practiced in renal transplants. The best possible match available is sought, and the crossmatch test must be negative. For bone marrow transplantation, an MHC identical family donor is ideal to reduce the likelihood of strong, possibly fatal, graft versus host reaction. However, the selection of negative MLC reactions in HLA nonidentical matches is facilitated by using DR typing and may facilitate the ease of matching and thus improve outcome.

Pathophysiology of Rejection

In this section, rejection of renal allografts is used as an example; however, the same principles apply to other types of allografts.

Components of the rejection process: The transplanted kidney or other tissue is rejected because transplantation antigens stimulate lymphocytes derived from primitive stem cells, eg, the T lymphocyte (which matures under the direct humoral influence of the thymus) and the B lymphocyte (which resembles the human equivalent of the cells of the avian bursa). Finally, the monocyte-macrophage system represents a pivotal intermediate and endstage effector. Although, at one time, T lymphocytes were held solely responsible for cellular allograft immunity and B lymphocytes for humoral immunity, it now appears that both types are necessary for graft rejection. Their cooperative action is mediated by the T cells after antigenic stimulation.

Mode of sensitization: The host may be sensitized in several ways by a renal allograft. B or T lymphocytes may be stimulated by (1) donor lymphocytes released from the kidney (passenger leukocytes), (2) subcellular antigen from the kidney liberated into the circulation, or (3) peripheral sensitization host lymphocytes that come in contact with donor antigens as they pass through the graft. Any or all of these mechanisms are probably operative. In general, T lymphocytes circulate in the peripheral blood and, together with monocytes, are predominantly responsible for cell-mediated immunity that includes allograft rejection by the nonsensitized recipient. On the other hand, B lymphocytes, produced in the bone marrow and found in both lymph nodes and spleen, are the precursors of cells that produce immunoglobulins (humoral antibody). A presensitized individual with high titers of cytotoxic antibody displays this kind of immunity.

Effector mechanisms: The interaction of sensitized T lymphocytes with antigen at the graft site triggers events that may result in eventual graft destruction. An early characteristic of renal allograft rejection is the perivascular accumulation and proliferation of large immature mononuclear cells. Migration inhibitory factor (MIF) may be synthesized, causing an accumulation of phagocytic cells that eventually migrate through the vessel wall. When circulating antibody fixes to graft cells during humoral rejection, the complement system is activated. Chemotactic factors are generated and attract polymorphonuclear leukocytes (PMN) to the site. Also, vascular endothelium is destroyed by antibody binding, complement activation, and platelet aggregates, which cause mechanical obstruction and lead to hypoxia, and by PMNs that release lysosomal enzymes. Eventually, fibrin is deposited on damaged blood vessel walls. At later stages, the partially damaged endothelial cells proliferate, and the fibrin, which is organized by fibroblasts, obliterates the lumen of the vessel and causes chronic graft ischemia.

Antigen-antibody complexes: Graft antigens of several specificities and antibody produced against these antigens may form soluble immune complexes that deposit on the vascular endothelium and injure it. This may produce the glomerular lesions seen in chronic renal transplant rejection.

Ischemia: The effect of these immunologic events upon the renal vasculature is clearly shown in Figures 64 and 65. Apparently, rejection is associated with ischemia, which is characterized by a decrease in total blood flow, disturbances in the intrarenal distribution of blood flow, decrease in glomerular filtration rate,

Figure 64
Normal renal microvasculature

Figure 65
Renal microvasculature during acute rejection

Note abundant supply of outer cortical vessels. These are illustrated by the perfusion of the organ with silicone and digestion of the surrounding tissue.

Note patchy perfusion of renal cortex. Dark areas represent tissue with no blood flow.

and decrease in effective renal plasma flow. In acute rejection, cortical ischemia resembles that following acute oliguric renal failure caused by shock, septic abortion, or mercuric chloride poisoning. The renal arteriogram shows marked decreases of cortical blood flow and a decrease in, or "pruning" of, the smaller cortical vessels. Rejection that proceeds at a slower rate produces a chronic diminution in renal blood flow, with slowly progressive vascular lesions that lead to glomerular and tubular atrophy and associated interstitial fibrosis. In hyperacute rejection, necrotizing vasculitis may occur, whereas in chronic allograft rejection, the vascular abnormalities tend to be obstructive and obliterative.

Other forms of parenchymal damage: Parenchymal damage in the rejected renal allograft is probably caused by microcirculatory aberrations that affect every part of the renal parenchyma. In vitro, sensitized lymphocytes can kill donor cells by direct contact, but we cannot be sure that direct contact between sensitized lymphocytes and the renal tubular cell causes

parenchymal damage. Possibly the interstitial process, in addition to ischemia, generates cytotoxic factors that lead to significant tubular damage (Figure 66). However, in heart allografts, an unknown mechanism causes rejection that is associated with cell-to-cell contact between infiltrating and parenchymal cells.

Clinical Types of Renal Allograft Rejection

Hyperacute rejection: This type of renal allograft rejection usually occurs within a few minutes to hours after transplantation and is a result of preformed cytotoxic antibodies that react with donor alloantigens and activate the complement system. As a result of this interaction, the kidney becomes swollen, blue, and mottled, and interstitial hemorrhage causes a pro-

Figure 66
Tubular damage in kidney

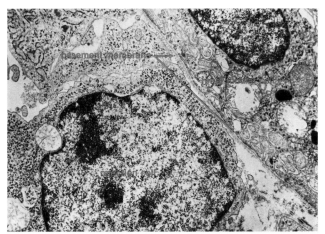

Electron micrograph indicates that death of an allografted kidney can be due to factors other than antibody or contact cytotoxicity. Lower left: Typical blast-like "rejection" cell has infiltrated renal cortex during acute rejection. Note large mitotically active nucleus and scanty cytoplasm containing numerous dispersed polyribosomes. The cell lacks a well-developed endoplasmic reticulum, suggesting that although it has actively proliferated in association with renal cell damage, it has not differentiated into a more mature antibody-producing plasma cell. Upper right: Degenerating renal tubular cell, presumably the end result of rejection. Note that intimate contact between the rejection cell and the degenerating parenchymal cell is prevented by the presence of tubular basement membrane.

Figure 67
Acute renal allograft rejection

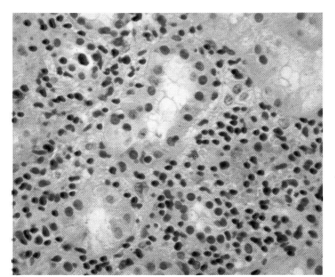

Note infiltration of mononuclear cells.

Figure 68
Treated renal allograft rejection

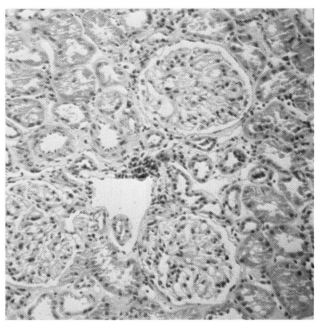

After a successfully treated rejection crisis, the inflammatory infiltrate clears.

found decrease in blood flow. In extreme cases, a rapidly progressive cortical necrosis occurs. Fibrinoid necrosis of afferent arterioles and thrombus formation with extensive endothelial injury are common. Symptoms include high fever, leukocytosis, and a swollen, tender kidney associated with anuria or oliguria. Also, the urine sediment shows numerous cellular elements, including desquamated tubular cells and red blood cells. At present, there is no successful therapy to terminate this chain of events.

Acute rejection: This is the usual form of rejection seen in the individual who has not been sensitized before receiving a transplant. Acute rejection is accompanied by a rapid decrease in renal function as revealed by a fall in urine output, rise in serum creatinine, enlargement and tenderness of the kidney, and not infrequently, hypertension. If properly treated, the "rejection crisis" is often reversible (Figures 67 and 68).

There is an acute mononuclear inflammatory response with perivascular accumulation of large immature mononuclear cells in the cortical interstitium. However, the vasculature is considerably less affected than in hyperacute rejection. Epithelial injury, platelet aggregation, and tubular necrosis may be seen. All these processes are reflected by decreased renal blood flow and glomerular filtration rate and, frequently, by an increase in hematuria and proteinuria (with red cell casts). There may be nonspecific signs of tissue destruction, such as increased urinary lysozyme excretion and increased serum lactic acid dehydrogenase concentration. A positive leukocyte migration-inhibition test, circulating cytotoxic T lymphocytes, and cytotoxic antibody reactive with B or T lymphocytes all occur during an acute transplantation rejection.

Chronic rejection: This type of rejection is seen in most unsuccessful human renal allografts that fail after months or years of good function. It is characterized by slowly progressive renal failure and frequently by hypertension. Histologic findings include endothelial proliferation of the small arteries and thickening of the glomerular basement membrane with eventual total hyalinization of glomeruli, interstitial fibrosis, and marked impairment of kidney function (Figure 69). Because the fibrotic disease does not respond to immunosuppressive therapy, such therapy should be kept to a minimum. During chronic rejection, lymphocyte-dependent antibody (LDA) may appear in the circulation. This antibody allows killer cells to destroy specific donor target cells in the absence of complement.

Glomerular disease in the renal allograft: As a result of the rejection process, glomerulonephritis may occur and may mimic any form of glomerular disease – frequently that of lobular glomerulonephritis with eventual hyalinization of the glomerulus. Unquestionably, the original glomerular disease afflicting the host may also recur in the transplanted kidney. Such unusual forms as nephritis accompanied by mesangial deposition of IgA, antiglomerular basement membrane nephritis, and systemic lupus erythematosus nephritis have recurred. These conditions do not necessarily lead to progressive failure of the renal allograft.

Figure 69
Chronic renal allograft rejection

(a)

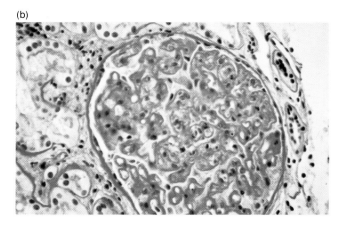

(b)

(c)

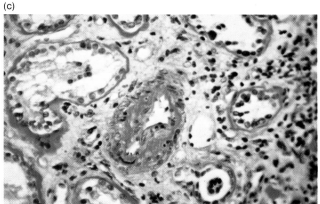

(a) Obliterative vascular lesion with breakdown of the elastic lamina. (b) Progressive glomerular lesion showing marked abnormalities in the structure of the basement membrane. (c) Note large amounts of fibrosis associated with tubular atrophy.

Allograft Prolongation

Chemical immunosuppression: In clinical practice, chemical immunosuppression prolongs survival of the transplanted organ. The most widely used drugs are azathioprine, cyclophosphamide, and corticosteroids (chapter 10). Fungal polypeptides, such as cyclosporin A, are being evaluated experimentally.

Natural tolerance: Naturally occurring immunologic tolerance was first demonstrated in adult fraternal-twin cattle whose blood contained cells from both twins. These dizygotic cattle shared common placental circulation before birth and presumably exchanged hematopoietic cells. Skin grafts can be successfully exchanged between chimeric cattle because they are immunologically tolerant of each other's transplantation antigens. A few human cases of true chimerism in fraternal twins have been documented.

Experimentally induced tolerance: The tolerant state is experimentally induced by injecting a fetal or neonatal mouse with the leukocytes of a subsequent tissue donor. In adult life, these neonatally treated animals accept tissue from the cell donor without evidence of rejection. Apparently, the introduction of foreign cells when the animal is immunologically immature permits the organism to recognize this foreign tissue as "self" (rather than as "foreign") and to become permanently tolerant due to central failure of the immune response. Subsequent studies showed that if sufficiently large doses of foreign cells were injected into immunologically mature animals, they became immunologically tolerant. More recently, it has been clearly demonstrated that a subthreshold dose of soluble antigen also renders an animal tolerant. Unfortunately, administration of minute amounts of soluble transplantation antigens has not yet produced true tolerance to tissue grafts.

The precise nature, mechanism(s), and significance of tolerance pose some fascinating problems of contemporary biology. Probably, under some experimental conditions, clonal deletion causes tolerance that can only be terminated by cell replacement. In other situations, specific suppressor cells may maintain the nonreactive state.

Intrinsic tolerance: Using donors of different histocompatibility genotypes, viable mice can be developed from pairs of conjoined, undifferentiated cleavage-state embryos. As adults, these "allophenic" mice are cellular mosaics in organ composition but are fully immunologically tolerant to tissue grafted from the original donor strains. They have a normal immune mechanism and do not develop any graft-versus-host disease or autoimmune phenomena. These truly tolerant animals are developed after conception but before differentiation of the immune system, thereby supporting a clonal selection hypothesis of immunologic development. In some instances, serum-blocking factors have been detected, suggesting that antibody or immune complexes or even suppressor cells may modulate the tolerant state or even lead to its development.

Enhancement: After immunization with foreign tissues, antibodies may be formed that prevent graft rejection. Sera that, when injected into normal animals, prolong the survival of tissue grafts are known as enhancing sera and contain enhancing antibody. Enhancing antibodies may coat the target graft (blocking) or combine with released antigen to form immune complexes that react with lymphoid cells and prevent the immune response (inhibition). Whether or not enhancing antibodies all belong to one immunoglobulin subclass is not yet established. It is theoretically possible to induce enhancing antibody in the recipient of an allograft. This approach, in the absence of well-defined and well-characterized enhancing sera for passive transfer, offers great promise for immunologically specific prevention of rejection.

Additionally, *suppressor* lymphocytes (a subpopulation of T lymphocytes) may be generated by alloantigen stimulation and may be a mechanism that prolongs an allograft. Also, following alloimmunization, suppressor cells with characteristics of monocytes have been described. The specific details of a method that will immunize a patient with transplantation antigens to induce a protective, rather than destructive, cellular immune response has not yet been found. It is encouraging, however, that enhancement can be induced against either type I or II antigens, and a response against the full antigen array is not necessary.

Figure 70
Graft-versus-host disease

a

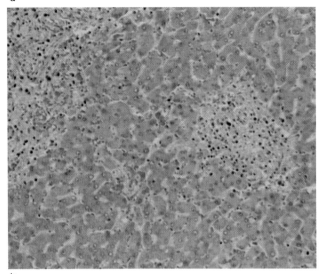

b

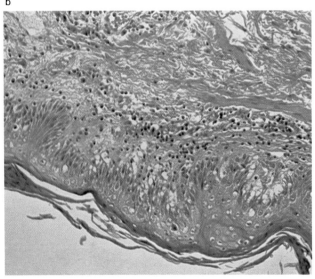

Graft-versus-host disease following human bone marrow transplantation. (a) Inflammatory infiltrate in portal regions of the liver. (b) An area of skin showing the nature of the inflammatory lesion. Note dermal mononuclear cell infiltrate.

In renal allograft recipients, an important clinical observation has been made: grafts survive longer in patients who have received multiple blood transfusions without becoming strongly sensitized. While the need for blood may be a marker for many clinical states and immunologic selection may have occurred, some of these patients who received many transfusions may have produced enhancing antibody or suppressor cells.

Graft adaptation: In graft recipients receiving nonspecific immunosuppressive agents, such as immunosuppressive drugs or antilymphocyte serum, certain "adaptations" may occur that render the graft less susceptible to immunologic destruction. Such a reduction in immunogenicity or graft adaptation has precedents in other areas. For example, serial passage of tumors alters the histocompatibility characteristics of the malignancy. Also, longstanding grafts are more difficult to destroy by injecting the recipient with sensitized lymphocytes than are recent transplants.

The mechanism of graft adaptation is unknown. However, it is probably related to the progressive loss of interstitial hematopoietically derived organ cells (passenger leukocytes) rather than to replacement of endothelium by host cells. This phenomenon explains why tissue allografts such as thyroid or islets of Langerhans are less immunogenic after a period of time in tissue culture.

Graft-versus-host reactions and bone marrow transplantation: If immunocompetent cells or hematopoietic stem cells, eg, bone marrow, are transplanted into an immunologically incompetent recipient, the transplanted cells will react with antigens present on recipient tissues and other target cells. The cell-cell interaction induces a proliferative and then an atrophic process that results in runting – a disease manifested by wasting, atrophy, diarrhea, dermatitis, infection, and ultimately death. These *graft-versus-host* reactions are a potential danger when lymphoid tissue containing immunologically competent cells or bone marrow is transplanted (Figure 70). To some extent, runting can be treated with cytotoxic drugs or antilymphocytic serum, both of which are sometimes used to prepare a recipient for a graft. Tissue matching, especially for the D locus, may minimize the disease. In the future, the problem will probably be conquered by tolerance induction or by preconditioning the recipient or cells of the bone marrow graft with specific antibody to suppress reactive clones.

After immunologic reconstitution with lymphoid tissue other than bone marrow, such as thymus or peripheral lymphocytes, it is particularly important to determine whether immune function is complete after transplantation. The altered self-hypothesis (see chapter 6) predicts that MHC restriction of some cooperative cellular responses would lead to an incompletely functioning immune system. In children with primary immune deficiency diseases following reconstitution, cellular collaboration between lymphocytes of different genotypes results in incomplete immune response when required for host defenses.

Transplantation of small numbers of bone marrow cells may be successful in certain immune deficiency diseases. To a lesser extent, grafts of large numbers of cells are successful in many cases of refractory aplastic anemia and to a lesser extent in leukemia.

The Future Prospects in Clinical Transplantation

Much excitement is now being generated by work on new immunosuppressive chemicals (prostaglandin analogues, fungal metabolites) and by new irradiation approaches (selective lymphoid irradiation, either directly or by isotopes). These approaches will soon undergo serious clinical evaluations. At the same time cardiac transplant programs are increasing, endocrine allografts, such as parathyroid and pancreas, are being undertaken clinically, and the important variables that influence the outcome of renal transplantation are becoming better understood. It is likely that during this decade problems of organ transplantation will be mastered.

Suggested Reading

Guttmann RD: Renal transplantation. *N Engl J Med 301*:975-982, 1038-1048, 1979.

HLA and Diseases

8

Introduction

The major human histocompatibility antigens (HLA) are involved in the etiology or pathogenesis of many diseases. Animal investigations showed that susceptibility to a variety of diseases was controlled by genes linked to the major histocompatibility system of the species. This linkage was first observed in some strains of mice that are especially susceptible to virus-induced leukemia, but susceptibility has also been demonstrated for toxoplasmosis, mammary tumor virus, autoimmune thyroiditis, and lymphocytic choriomeningitis virus. In the mouse, *immune response genes* (Ir genes) determine an individual's capacity to respond to a particular antigen. Ir genes, which are located in the major histocompatibility complex (MHC), additionally control a variety of regulatory interactions among T lymphocytes, B lymphocytes, and macrophages. These animal studies stimulated a search for a similar relationship between histocompatibility antigens and human diseases.

Before describing the numerous associations already known between HLA and disease, it is necessary to review briefly the genetics of the HLA system.

The HLA gene complex is located on the short arm of chromosome 6 (Figure 71). At least five closely linked but distinct genes (loci) are known (A, B, C, D and DR), each of which has many different alleles (Tables 19, 20, 21). The particular combination of alleles at each locus on the same chromosome is called the haplotype; two haplotypes, one from each parent, constitute the genotype. In most families, the genes on a particular haplotype are always inherited together. However, on rare occasions, recombination may occur.

The HLA antigens are glycoproteins floating in the plasma membrane of most nucleated cells. They are detected serologically by means of cytotoxicity assays, using peripheral blood lymphocytes as targets (see chapter 6). Although HLA-A, -B, and -C antigens are found on all nucleated cells (except erythrocytes), HLA-D and DR antigens exist only on B lymphocytes, monocytes, epidermal and endothelial cells.

The HLA-D antigens are identified by means of the mixed lymphocyte reaction. Closely associated with the HLA-D locus antigens are a group of HLA-DR antigens, which are detected serologically on B lymphocytes (Table 21). Other genes that code for complement factors 2 and 4 and for the properdin factor (Bf) are closely linked to the HLA complex.

The concept of *linkage disequilibrium*, which postulates that some haplotypes occur more or less often than would be expected by chance, is important in many of the proposed explanations for the association between diseases and HLA. For instance, in Caucasians the HLA haplotypes A1, B8, Dw3 and A3, B7, Dw2 occur more often than the product of the individual frequencies of these alleles. Linkage disequilibrium could result from natural selection, ie, a selective advantage existing for some haplotypic antigen combinations.

There are two different types of relationships between the HLA system and diseases. One type is *association*, which is revealed by population studies in which the frequencies of HLA antigens in unrelated patients are compared with those of healthy controls. The association of HLA-B27 with ankylosing spondylitis was discovered by observing that B27 occurs much more often in patients with this disorder than in healthy individuals. The other possible type, genetic *linkage*, is recognized by family studies showing that affected relatives share HLA haplotypes more often than expected according to genetic laws. Such family studies show that congenital adrenal hyperplasia is transmitted in linkage with the HLA system.

Because quantitative measures of the strength of HLA and disease associations are needed, the concept of *relative risk* (RR) was developed. The relative risk, obtained by a simple calculation, represents the risk of developing a disease in an individual possessing a particular HLA antigen compared to an individual lacking that antigen.

Diseases reported to be associated with specific HLA antigens have certain general features in common. They are usually of unknown, possibly viral, etiology. They are often hereditary diseases but with weak penetrance. Many are characterized by immunological abnormalities with autoantibodies or by cellular infiltration into the lesions. Their evolution is usually subacute or chronic but with little impact on reproduction. Most associations found so far have been with antigens coded by the HLA-B and -D or DR loci (Table 22).

Figure 71
Schematic comparison of the genetic maps of the mouse H-2 and human HLA regions

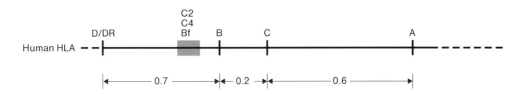

The letters above the line indicate loci or regions. Ss stands for serum substance and is now known to be a gene for the fourth component of complement C4. H-2G, Q, and TL are, respectively, loci for red-cell blood groups, antigens expressed on thymocytes and some lymph-node cells, and a series of antigens expressed also on thymocytes and certain thymic leukemias. I represents the region containing several immune-response loci as well as loci controlling the mixed lymphocyte culture response and the Ia (immune-associated) antigens. C2, C4, and Bf refer to the second and fourth factors of the classical complement pathway and factor B of the alternative pathway. The numbers underneath the line for HLA are the approximate percentage recombination fractions.

Table 19
HLA-A, -B and -C locus gene frequencies (percent)

Allele	European Caucasoids (228)*	African Blacks (102)	Japanese (195)	Allele	European Caucasoids (228)*	African Blacks (102)	Japanese (195)
A1	15.8	3.9	1.2	B18	6.2	2.0	–
A2	27.0	9.4	25.3	B27	4.6	–	0.3
A3	12.6	6.4	0.7	B15	4.8	3.0	9.3
Aw23 (9)	2.4	10.8	–	Bw38 (w16)	2.0	–	1.8
Aw24 (9)	8.8	2.4	36.7	Bw39 (w16)	3.5	1.5	4.7
A25 (10)	2.0	3.5	–	B17	5.7	16.1	0.6
A26 (10)	3.9	4.5	12.7	Bw21	2.2	1.5	1.5
A11	5.1	–†	6.7	Bw22	3.6	–	6.5
A28	4.4	8.9	–	Bw35	9.9	7.2	9.4
A29	5.8	6.4	0.2	B37	1.1	–	0.8
Aw30	3.9	22.1	0.5	B40	8.1	2.0	21.8
Aw31	2.3	4.2	8.7	Bw41	1.2	1.5	–
Aw32	2.9	1.5	0.5	Bw42	–	12.3	–
Aw33	0.7	1.0	2.0	Blank	2.4	17.9	7.6
Aw43	–	4.0	–	Cw1	4.8	–	11.1
Blank	2.2	11.0	4.2	Cw2	5.4	11.4	1.4
B5	5.9	3.0	20.9	Cw3	9.4	5.5	26.3
B7	10.4	7.3	7.1	Cw4	12.6	14.2	4.3
B8	9.2	7.1	0.2	Cw5	8.4	1.0	1.2
B12	16.6	12.7	6.5	Cw6	12.6	17.7	2.1
B13	3.2	1.5	0.8	Blank	46.7	50.2	53.5
B14	2.4	3.6	0.5				

The data in this Table and Tables 20, 21 are taken from the
Seventh Workshop (Bodmer *et al,* 1978).

*Numbers tested
†Alleles indicated thus – are not present in this population.

Tables 19, 20, and 21 reproduced with permission from the Medical Department,
The British Council.

Table 20
HLA-D locus gene frequencies (percent)

Allele	European Caucasoids (99)*	North American Caucasoids (125)
Dw1	7.9	6.8
Dw2	9.5	11.7
Dw3	9.5	9.0
Dw4	5.1	5.2
Dw5	9.0	6.1
Dw6	11.5	8.9
Dw7	5.8	9.8
Dw8	2.5	1.6
Blank	39.1	40.9

*Number tested

Table 21
HLA-DR locus gene frequencies (percent)
in different populations

Allele	European Caucasoids (334)*	African Blacks (77)	Japanese (164)
DR1	6.2	—†	4.5
DR2	11.2	8.7	16.5
DR3	8.9	11.7	—
DR4	7.8	3.5	14.4
DR5	15.1	7.4	5.4
DRw6	8.6	9.9	6.7
DR7	15.6	6.6	—
DRw8	5.6	7.2	7.2
Blank	21.1	45.0	45.3

*Numbers tested
†Alleles indicated thus — are not present in this population.

Table 22
Association between HLA and disease

Disease	Antigen	Antigen frequency (percent) Patients	Control	Relative risk
Rheumatic diseases				
Ankylosing spondylitis				
Caucasians	B27	79-100	4-13	87.4
Japanese	B27	67-92	0-2	324.5
Haida Indians	B27	100	51	34.4
American Blacks	B27	48	2	36.5
Reiter's syndrome	B27	65-100	4-19	37
Yersinia arthritis	B27	58-76	9-14	17.6
Salmonella arthritis	B27	60-92	8-14	29.7
Psoriatic arthritis	B27	17-61	4-14	10.7
Juvenile rheumatoid arthritis	B27	15-57	6-14	4.5
Rheumatoid arthritis	DR4	70	28	5.8
Immunopathological diseases				
Systemic lupus erythematosus	DR2	57	26	4
	DR3	46	22	3
Sjögren syndrome	DR3	68-69	10-24	9.7
Graves' disease				
Caucasians	Dw3	50-54	4-26	3.7
Japanese	Bw35	0-57	5-20	3.9
Hashimoto's disease	DR3	55	26	3.4
Addison disease	Dw3	70	26	6.3
Juvenile diabetes	Dw3	30-46	19-26	2.2
	Dw4	48-52	18-19	4.0
Myasthenia gravis (female less than 35 yrs)	Dw3	76	19	12.7
Chronic active hepatitis	DR3	68	24	6.6
Gluten-sensitive enteropathy	Dw3	63-93	22-27	10.8
Dermatitis herpetiformis	Dw3	74-92	22-26	15.4
Malignant diseases				
Hodgkin disease	A1	29-62	20-49	1.4
	B8	11-35	12-33	1.2
Acute lymphoblastic leukemia	A2	46-68	37-60	1.4
	B12	17-75	16-36	1.2

Table 22 continued

Disease	Antigen	Antigen frequency (percent)		Relative risk
		Patients	Control	
Miscellaneous diseases				
Multiple sclerosis	Dw2	47-68	18-32	4.0
de Quervain syndrome	Bw35	63-73	9-21	13.7
Behçet disease	B5	12-86	9-27	6.3
Buerger disease	B12	0-2	28-30	0.08
Goodpasture's syndrome	DR2	88	32	13.1
Takayasu's disease	B52	44	13	5.4
Haemochromatosis	A3	60-100	18-31	8.2
	B7	34-83	19-34	3.0
	B14	17-29	3-12	4.7
Pemphigus vulgaris	DR4	90-91	25-38	31.5
Idiopathic membranous nephropathy	DR3	75-76	20-23	12.0
Psoriasis	Cw6	50	7	13.2

Figure 72
B27 and ankylosing spondylitis.

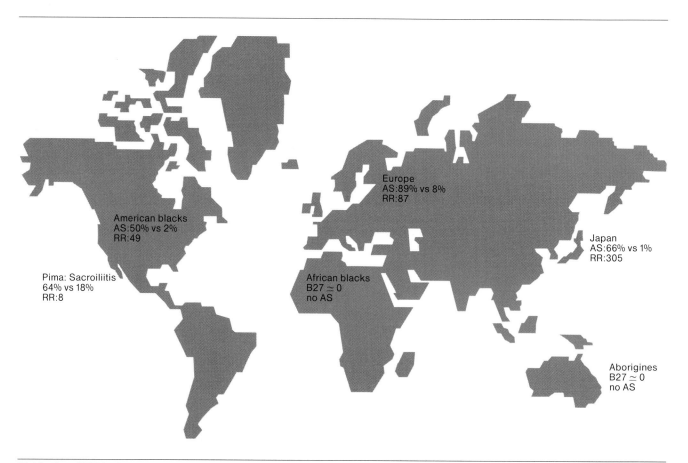

Distribution of B27 in the world. B27 is practically absent in the
population of the southern hemisphere. The frequencies of B27 in
ankylosing spondylitis (AS) or sacroiliitis patients versus controls are
given for some populations, as well as the relative risk (RR).

Associations Between HLA and Disease

Rheumatic diseases: The best known of these associations and the most striking to date is between B27 and *ankylosing spondylitis*, a seronegative arthritis of unknown etiology occurring predominantly in males and affecting the lumbodorsal spine, the sacroiliac, and sometimes the peripheral joints. In the Caucasian population, B27 is present in 85% to 95% of patients compared to only 6% to 10% of control populations (Figure 72). B27 is also associated with the disease in other ethnic groups such as the Japanese or the American blacks, despite a low frequency of B27 in these populations. Neither B27 nor ankylosing spondylitis is present in African blacks and Australian aborigines. By contrast, in British Columbia 10% of the adult male Haida Indians have sacroiliitis, whereas the frequency of B27 is 51% in the Haida population and 100% in the few ankylosing spondylitis patients tested. For individuals with B27, the relative risk of ankylosing spondylitis is about 200 times that of B27-negative individuals. It has been estimated that the disease will develop in 20% of individuals with B27 and that the prevalence of ankylosing spondylitis is much higher than generally accepted.

In addition to ankylosing spondylitis, the frequency of B27 is increased in a large group of patients with other types of arthritis: Reiter's syndrome, acute anterior uveitis, juvenile rheumatoid arthritis, and acute arthritis following specific infections such as *Salmonella*, *Shigella* or *Yersinia*. Although different pathogens seem responsible for each of these diseases, they probably have a common pathogenetic mechanism involving perhaps B27 directly or a closely linked susceptibility gene. Evidence is accumulating for immunological crossreactivity between B27 and an antigen in gram-negative bacteria.

Unlike the other forms of arthritis, adult rheumatoid arthritis is not associated with B27 but with HLA-Dw4. The fact that rheumatoid arthritis has a susceptibility gene different from the other forms of arthritis suggests that this disorder is probably a distinct disease. The absence of a strong familial incidence of rheumatoid arthritis suggests that environmental factors override genetic susceptibility.

Immunopathological diseases: The hypothesis that disease associations with the HLA system may indicate the existence of abnormal immune-response genes stimulated the study of HLA antigens in autoimmune diseases. Many of these disorders, which are characterized by abnormalities of the immune response, chronic inflammation, and autoantibody formation, are associated with an increased frequency of the antigens B8 and Dw3, which are known to be in linkage disequilibrium. Studies of immune responses of normal individuals or patients possessing these two antigens show stronger responsiveness in mixed lymphocyte culture, higher antibody titers against bacterial antigens, and higher frequency of autoantibodies than controls not possessing these antigens. In addition, kidney transplant recipients who possess B8 reject incompatible grafts more readily than recipients without B8.

Systemic lupus erythematosus is a disease characterized by a pleomorphic clinical picture; skin, joints, kidney, heart, nervous system, and respiratory tract are affected. The most important biological feature is the presence of antibodies to native DNA, although many other autoantibodies are found. Viruses have been suspected as the etiologic agents in a genetically susceptible host. Two HLA-DR antigens (DR2 and DR3) are associated with systemic lupus erythematosus, whereas HLA-B8 is only slightly increased. Thus, it seems that at least two independent genes determine autoimmunity in this disease.

Sjögren syndrome, which occurs mostly in females, is a combination of rheumatoid joint disease and dryness of the eyes and mouth. This disorder is also associated with HLA-B8 and DR3, but again the association with the D-locus antigen is stronger than that with the B-locus antigen. The same two antigens, B8 and DR3, have been found with increased frequency in patients with various chronic endocrinopathies, such as *Graves' disease, Hashimoto's thyroiditis, Addison disease* and *insulin-dependent diabetes mellitus*. All of these diseases are associated with autoantibody formation and lymphocyte infiltration with inflammation of the target endocrine organs. However, although *pernicious anemia* is clinically associated with the latter three disorders, there is a normal frequency of HLA-B8 or -DR3.

Interestingly, B8 is virtually absent in the Japanese population, and there Graves' disease is associated with Bw35, and insulin-dependent diabetes mellitus with Bw54. This suggests that it is not the HLA genes themselves but rather other genes closely linked to the HLA genes that play a role in the development of these diseases.

Insulin-dependent diabetes mellitus is not only associated with B8 and Dw3 but also with B15 and Dw4, two determinants that are also in linkage disequilibrium. As with most other disease-associated antigens, individuals homozygous for either of these antigens appear to have the same relative risk as individuals possessing only a single dose of the antigen, ie, no gene-dose effect is observed. Individuals who carry both Dw3 and Dw4, however, have about twice the risk of developing the disease as those who carry either antigen alone. This additive effect indicates that HLA-Dw3 and HLA-Dw4 confer susceptibility to diabetes by different mechanisms. Non-insulin-dependent diabetes mellitus is not associated with HLA.

Myasthenia gravis, a disease of neuromuscular transmission producing muscle weakness and fatigability, is associated with thymic abnormalities and autoantibody formation. In about 50% of patients, B8 and Dw3 have been found. Two forms of myasthenia gravis may exist. One has a high frequency of B8 and Dw3 and is characterized by early age at onset, prevalence in females, thymic hyperplasia, and a low incidence of antibodies against skeletal muscle. The other form of myasthenia gravis is characterized by adult onset, male predominance, thymoma, and a high incidence of autoantibodies; it is not associated with B8 and Dw3.

Chronic active hepatitis, another disorder with typical autoimmune histological and serological features, is associated with HLA-A1, -B8, and -Dw3. Because of the significantly greater frequency of Dw3, the association with the A and B loci is thought to be an indirect result of association with Dw3. A subgroup of this disorder, which is associated with hepatitis B surface antigen in blood, does not appear to be associated with any HLA antigen. Interestingly, in a haemodialysis population, HLA-B8 is associated with the capacity to eliminate HBs Ag from the blood, suggesting that this genotype may confer strong immune response to certain viral antigens.

Gluten-sensitive enteropathy (celiac sprue), a disease of the mucosa of the small intestine, is caused by gluten sensitivity. Gluten is not toxic by itself, but it causes an immune cytotoxic reaction directed at intestinal epithelial cells, which leads to malabsorption. Sixty to eighty percent of patients with gluten sensitivity possess antigens B8 and Dw3. As in the case of other immunopathological diseases mentioned before, it seems that the D-locus antigen is more highly correlated with gluten-sensitive enteropathy than with the B-locus antigen. This suggests that the susceptibility gene is more closely linked to the D locus.

Dermatitis herpetiformis is a pruritic vesicular skin disease frequently associated with gluten-sensitive enteropathy. The skin lesions contain IgA immunoglobulins, probably in the form of gliadin-antigliadin complexes. As in gluten-sensitive enteropathy, patients have a high frequency of HLA-B8 and Dw3.

Thus, a number of autoimmune diseases are associated with HLA-B8, and most of them show an even stronger association with Dw3 and DR3. It is unclear whether each of these disorders is associated with a different gene, all in linkage disequilibrium with B8 and Dw3, or whether all diseases are associated with the same susceptibility gene or immune response gene.

Malignant diseases: Genes within the major histocompatibility complex influence survival of inbred strains of mice with virus-induced leukemia. The associations between the HLA antigens and human malignant diseases are weaker than those between the nonmalignant immunopathological diseases and HLA. In Hodgkin disease, antigens A1 and B8 have a higher incidence in patients who have survived more than five years than in the patients who have been treated for less than one year. This difference may be due to a resistance factor associated with this haplotype. The A1, B8, Dw3 haplotype is associated with enhanced immunological responsiveness, and it is possible that the same mechanism is responsible for its influence on survival in Hodgkin disease. In childhood acute lymphoblastic leukemia (ALL), the long-term survivors have a high frequency of HLA-A2. This antigen may confer an increased resistance to the disease. In most of the other forms of cancer, no convincing HLA associations have been so far observed. However, in two distinct malignant disorders, nasopharyngeal carcinoma and esophageal carcinoma, relatively close associations with HLA antigens have been described. In nasopharyngeal carcinoma, which occurs with an unusually high frequency in Chinese, there is an increased frequency of Bw46. Esophageal carcinoma seems to have an association with Bw40 in Turkish-Mongol people, among whom the disease incidence is unusually high.

Miscellaneous diseases: *Multiple sclerosis* is characterized by many patches of demyelination in the central nervous system, which causes a debilitating, wasting disease. In the Caucasian population, multiple sclerosis is associated with antigens B7, Dw2, and DR2. Patients possessing Dw2 have a more severe and unremitting course than the patients without Dw2. Although Dw2 is rare in American blacks, its frequency is increased in black patients with multiple sclerosis. However, in other populations, different antigens are involved, eg, DR5 in Japanese and DR4 in Arabs. It is likely, therefore, that these HLA genes are in linkage disequilibrium with a susceptibility gene or an immune-response gene more directly concerned with the initiation of the disease.

de Quervain syndrome, a subacute thyroiditis following mumps, is associated with Bw35 and Cw4. This may be another disease that is induced by a viral infection and in which an immune-response gene may play an important role.

Behçet disease is a chronic syndrome of unknown cause with recurring ulcers, iridocyclitis, conjunctivitis, and uveitis. The frequency of B5 is high in both Caucasians and Japanese patients (Figure 73).

Buerger disease, a form of arteriosclerosis prevalent in some ethnic groups, reveals a marked decreased frequency of B12. This disorder may provide a clue to the existence of resistance genes linked to the HLA system.

Hemochromatosis, a genetic disorder characterized by abnormal intestinal absorption of iron, is the only disease presently known that is associated with an HLA-A locus antigen, A3, often with one or both of two specific haplotypes: A3, B7 and A3, B14. It is possible that these two haplotypes segregate with one of the genes, which leads to excessive accumulation of iron.

Figure 73
Pedigree of an Israeli family with Behçet disease

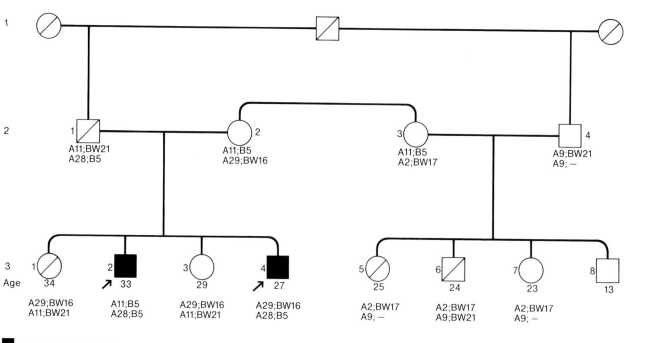

■ Male, Behçet disease

⊘ Female, aphthous stomatitis

↗ Proband

Figure 74
Genetic mapping of the 21-hydroxylase-deficiency gene within the HLA linkage group

Family Zurich 7 (21-hydroxylase deficiency)

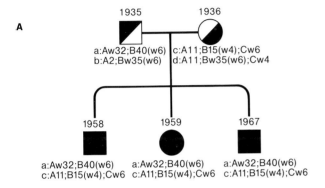

Family N.Y. 16 (21-hydroxylase deficiency)

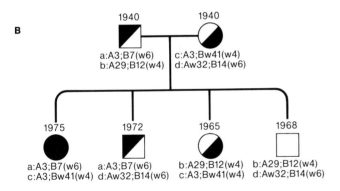

The HLA haplotypes for the HLA-A, HLA-B and HLA-C alleles are given in each family. The paternal haplotypes are labeled a and b, and the maternal haplotypes c and d. The parents are obligate heterozygous carriers for the 21-hydroxylase-deficiency gene (denoted by half-black symbols). The affected children are denoted by black symbols.

In A, three affected siblings are HLA genotypically identical. In B, one affected child is HLA genotypically different from the three unaffected siblings. One sibling who carries the parental a and d haplotypes is probably a heterozygous carrier for 21-hydroxylase deficiency and shares the a haplotype with the patient. Another sibling has the parental b and c haplotypes and shares the c haplotype with the patient and should be a carrier of the 21-hydroxylase deficiency gene. The child with the b and d haplotypes should be normal for the gene.

Psoriasis is the only disease that is clearly associated with the HLA-C locus. A striking association with CW6 and with B13 and B17, which show linkage disequilibrium with CW6, has been observed among Caucasians, Japanese, and the Ashkenaz Jews.

Diseases Linked to the HLA System

Several disorders are linked to the HLA region on chromosome 6. In the population as a whole, they are not associated with any particular HLA antigens, but within a single family, they are associated with a haplotype. Hypersensitivity to ragweed pollen and other allergens appears to be linked to HLA in some families but not in others. At least two different genetic regions control allergic diseases: one is linked to HLA and controls the specific immune response, and one is not linked to HLA and controls the level of IgE. This is the evidence, albeit sparse, in human beings for the existence of immune-response genes. Another example of linkage of a genetic defect with HLA is the deficiency of specific proteins of the complement system. C4 deficiency is controlled by genetic determinants closely linked to the HLA complex; C2 deficiency is linked to the haplotype A25, B18, Dw2 and can be mapped close to the HLA-D locus. The other deficiencies in complement components do not seem to be linked with the HLA complex.

Congenital adrenal hyperplasia is an autosomal recessive disease that is associated in most cases with steroid 21-hydroxylase deficiency. Family studies have shown that the gene responsible segregates with the HLA haplotypes (Figure 74), and there is some evidence for an association with HLA-Bw47.

Possible Pathogenetic Mechanisms of HLA and Disease

Two hypotheses account for the associations between HLA and diseases. The first postulates that the HLA antigens are involved in the pathogenetic mechanism. The second implicates some unidentified immune response genes that are associated with HLA through linkage disequilibrium.

Direct relationship between HLA antigens and susceptibility to diseases: HLA antigens may function as cell-surface receptors for viruses, toxins, or hormones. The only human example of a receptor role for cell membrane antigens involves the Duffy erythrocyte antigen, which is essential for the penetration of malarial parasites into erythrocytes. The hypothesis of "molecular mimicry" postulates that a virus or toxin may share antigenic configurations with the host's HLA antigen. As a result, the host is tolerant to these cross-reacting determinants and unable to mount an immune response against the microorganisms. Some evidence favors cross-reactivity between B27 and gram-negative bacteria such as *Klebsiella*. HLA antigens may also be incorporated into the protein coat of viruses budding from the cell surface. Such viruses can then easily infect another host that shares the same HLA antigens. The direct involvement of HLA antigens is an attractive hypothesis and could explain associations with diseases in which viral or other microbial agents are implicated. However, it is unlikely to account for many other associations, particularly diseases in which an associated antigen is present only in half the patients or in which more than one HLA antigen is associated with a single disease.

Effect of an immune-response gene linked to HLA: Associations between HLA and disease may reflect the existence of disease-susceptibility genes or abnormal immune-response genes that are closely linked to, but not identical to, the genes producing HLA antigens. This explanation is attractive because the HLA loci represent only a small fraction of the genes in this chromosomal region and because linkage disequilibrium is a well-established characteristic of this complex. Also, a viral infection in mice presents strong supporting evidence for this hypothesis. The disease associated with lymphocytic choriomeningitis virus in mice is caused by the host's immune response. The ability to mount this immunological response is under the control of genes closely linked with the major histocompatibility complex. Mice that have a deficient cell-mediated immune system survive. Although the existence of immune response genes in man has not yet been conclusively demonstrated, it is likely that they influence the course of many infections.

Abnormalities in structural genes for complement components may also affect disease susceptibility. It seems likely that immunopathological diseases, which are associated with B8 and more strongly with Dw3, are caused by abnormal immune-response genes that are closely linked with HLA-D.

Clinical and Practical Implications

Discovery of the associations between HLA and diseases has permitted a better classification of some disorders. In the case of the arthritic disorders associated with B27, a common genetic denominator has been established for diseases that were previously linked only by clinical observations. Conversely, subdivisions of diseases have been made possible through HLA associations. Myasthenia gravis is divided into two distinct forms: one with thymus hyperplasia associated with Dw3; the other with thymoma and antimuscle antibody. Insulin-dependent diabetes, associated with Dw3 and Dw4, has been clearly distinguished from insulin-independent diabetes of adults that is not associated with HLA. There are only a few instances where HLA typing has been useful in diagnosing human diseases. Because of its exceptional strength, the B27 association with the incomplete forms of ankylosing spondylitis has helped the rheumatologist make the correct diagnosis. However, HLA typing has so far been of little value in the diagnosis and the management of other diseases. On the other hand, in families already afflicted by a particular disease, the diagnostic interest becomes more important. Susceptible children can be detected early, and in hemochromatosis, for instance, treatment by bleeding and the use of chelating chemicals can be initiated early. Another potential use of HLA typing might be the prenatal diagnosis of diseases linked with HLA, such as congenital adrenal hyperplasia. If diagnosis of the latter disease by the HLA typing of amniotic cells taken in the second trimester of pregnancy proves possible, it will allow parents with a previously affected child to consider selective abortion. For genetic counseling, HLA typing could potentially assess risks for serious hereditary diseases (insulin-dependent diabetes, hemochromatosis, ankylosing spondylitis, and multiple sclerosis). On the prognostic level, HLA typing may be helpful. For instance, it has been shown that Dw2-positive patients with multiple sclerosis have a more severe, unremitting course than those patients who are Dw2-negative. Also, in chronic active hepatitis, response to treatment is significantly worse in patients with HLA-Dw3 than in patients who lack this antigen. Patients who are homozygous for the predisposing antigen seem to suffer from a more severe form of some diseases, eg, myasthenia gravis, chronic active hepatitis, and ankylosing spondylitis.

It is possible that in polygenic illness, markers of several susceptibility genes will be found in the same disease. The coexistence of two markers in the same individual will then have a high prognostic value. The impact of these studies on preventive medicine can be easily foreseen. Until now, preventive medicine has been indiscriminate; with HLA typing, it may become more specific, less expensive, and more efficient.

Selected Bibliography

Dausset J and Svejgaard A: HLA and disease. Williams and Wilkins, Baltimore, 1977.

Dick HM: HLA and disease: Introductory Review. *Br Med Bull 34*:271, 1978.

Festenstein H and Demant P: HLA and H-2 Basic Immunogenetics, Biology and Clinical Relevance. Edward Arnold, Ltd., London.

Ryder LP, Anderson E, Svejgaard A: HLA and Disease Registry, Third Report. Copenhagen, Munksgaard, 1979.

Sasazuki T, McDevitt HO, Grumet FC: The association between genes in the major histocompatibility complex and disease susceptibility. *Annu Rev Med 28*:452, 1977.

Schaller JG and Omenn GS: The histocompatibility system and human disease. *J Pediatr 88*:913, 1976.

Introduction

The success with which the immune system is mobilized against many infectious diseases proves that it is a natural defense mechanism that can be instructed and controlled. The observation that some experimental tumors are antigenic *suggests* that the immune system could even be directed against malignancy. Our ability to inhibit the immune response to permit successful organ transplantation implies that we could also do the opposite and augment it to combat neoplastic growth. Although the immune mechanisms involved in transplantation and tumor rejection seem to be the same, the growing cancer has proven to be a more formidable adversary, and success has been very limited. We are now faced with the possibilities that many tumors are not antigenic (although some may be antigenic but not sufficiently to be immunogenic), that tumors are unlike normal tissue and may be able to fight back, and that the immune response is ambivalent or even negligent in dealing with malignancy. This chapter summarizes our current understanding of the interactions between malignant tumors and the immune system and describes some of the steps that are being taken to try to augment immune resistance to cancer.

Malignant Cell Antigens

Of all cell structures that may be altered in malignancy, the cell surface is one of the most important. Changes in the cell membrane may alter the uptake and release of materials and alter adhesiveness and cohesiveness in ways that lead to invasion and metastasis. Changes in cell-surface antigens are reflected not only by modification of the normal antigens but also by the formation of new tumor-specific antigens. Although such tumor-specific antigens are not confined to the surface, it is on the intact cell that they are most readily detected. Moreover, the tumor specific transplantation antigens (TSTA) – expressed on the surface of the cell – are responsible for, and sensitive to, the immune response; they may be the antigens that are responsible for tumor rejection.

Normal and Tumor-Specific Transplantation Antigens

Malignancy appears to reduce the number of normal transplantation antigens, particularly if the tumor cell has lost most of its biological specificity and has reverted to an undifferentiated form. The representation of the normal transplantation antigens is reduced on the surface of a tumor cell (H-2 antigens in the mouse, HLA in humans – antigens determined by the major histocompatibility loci), although none is completely absent. In addition, the tumor cell may show new antigenic specificities not present on the normal adult cell (Figure 75), though some may be found on fetal cells. Experimental tumors showing tumor-specific transplantation antigens include all the virus-induced tumors, many tumors induced by chemical carcinogens, and some induced by physical agents – but very few spontaneous tumors. Little is known about the structure of most of these antigens.

Virus-induced tumors: Although the DNA tumor-inducing viruses are among the smallest known, they are large enough to code for about six new proteins in any infected cell. Most of the proteins coded by these small viruses are (as expected) new, antigenic, and different from native cellular material. Not all of these new proteins, however, are present on the surface of the cell as new transplantation antigens; some are necessary for the synthesis and structure of new virus particles (Figure 76). Of potential significance in the study of human malignancy is the fact that all experimental tumors induced by any one virus contain the same new tumor-specific antigens. Tumors induced by different viruses have different antigens, although they may share some antigens with other tumors induced by closely related viruses. This is particularly true of the RNA viruses, which are considerably larger than most of the DNA viruses. Many tumor viruses are highly oncogenic in one species but produce few or no tumors in another. Paradoxically, these viruses are usually least oncogenic in their natural host species. A proposed explanation of this anomaly follows.

Tumors induced by chemical carcinogens: Chemical carcinogens appear to interact almost randomly with cellular DNA, producing some tumors that are highly antigenic, others less so, and some not at all. Tumors that appear after a short latent period are more apt to be antigenic than those that appear later, perhaps because immune selection destroys the most antigenic tumor cells. Moreover, tumors that are antigenic show

Figure 75
Surface antigens in malignancy

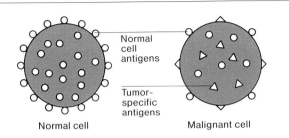

Normal cell antigens

Tumor-specific antigens

Normal cell   Malignant cell

Normal surface antigens may be reduced in malignancy; none are completely missing. New tumor-specific antigens may appear.

Figure 76
Malignant transformation of a normal cell by an oncogenic virus

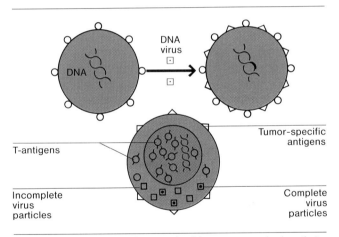

DNA

DNA virus

T-antigens

Tumor-specific antigens

Incomplete virus particles

Complete virus particles

Malignant transformation of a normal cell by an oncogenic virus that may affect the same cell type of different species by coding a new tumor-specific surface antigen. Bottom: Three new antigens in a virus transformed cell. Virus capsid antigen and new virus particles may be found in the malignant transformed cell previously infected and destined to undergo lysis.

a high degree of individual specificity. Two tumors induced in the same animal by the same chemical may be antigenically different (Figure 77). It is not known if these tumors are antigenically homogeneous, if they are made up of cells with several different antigens each, or if they are composed of a heterogeneous assortment of cells that are antigenically different from each other. Neither is it known whether the antigenic profile of the population of cells is stable or if it changes with time, as do many other properties of such tumors. Recent studies show that some tumors induced by chemical carcinogens also show common, cross-reacting antigens, some of which are embryonic in nature.

Spontaneous tumors: In experimental systems, tumors that are caused neither by oncogenic viruses nor by chemical carcinogens are considered to be spontaneous tumors. Most of these tumors are not immunogenic, so they do not induce resistance to tumor growth. Limited by our knowledge of the causes of cancer in humans, we must assume that some, and perhaps many, human tumors are also spontaneous and possibly not immunogenic.

Carcinoembryonic antigens (CEA): Another source of tumor antigens are the carcinoembryonic antigens that are coded by the DNA of the cell (Figure 78). Although not strictly tumor specific, these "tumor-associated" antigens may be absent from normal adult cells or present only in small quantities. As originally demonstrated in human gastrointestinal malignancies, the carcinoembryonic antigens appear to be normal components of fetal cells. During later development, these antigens are repressed, only to reappear in cells undergoing malignant changes, presumably as a result of derepression and reexpression of fetal genes. Sera from patients with malignancies of the GI tract frequently contain fetal antigens that were at one time thought to be diagnostic of gastrointestinal malignancies. It has subsequently been shown that such antigens are found in the circulation of patients with a variety of other malignant tumors and also in patients with nonmalignant diseases of the gastrointestinal tract. Thus, the use of carcinoembryonic antigen levels as a screening test for malignancy is not feasible. However, rising serum levels of CEA appear to be significant and may be useful in detecting recurrent disease.

Figure 77
Tumor antigens induced by chemical carcinogens

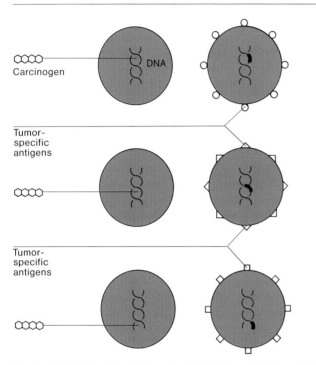

Carcinogen — DNA

Tumor-specific antigens

Tumor-specific antigens

When cells of identical genetic background are transformed with the same chemical carcinogen, each new tumor has its own antigenic specificity that is not shared with other tumors.

Figure 78
Carcinoembryonic antigen

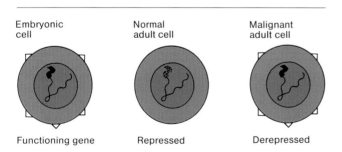

Embryonic cell	Normal adult cell	Malignant adult cell
Functioning gene	Repressed	Derepressed

(1) An embryonic cell shows a functioning gene that produced a normal embryonic antigen. (2) A normal adult cell shows the gene as a dotted line in the chromosome and no antigen on the surface of the cell. This indicates that the gene has been repressed in the normal adult cell. (3) A malignant adult cell shows the gene back in its active form, and the embryonic antigen, now called a carcinoembryonic antigen, is again present on the surface of the cell.

The Immune Response

Experimentally, the ultimate criterion of immunity is rejection of transplanted tumors by preimmunized animals. Inbred animals of identical genetic background usually are used to avoid the complicating factors of immunity developed against normal transplantation antigens. These antigenic tumors induce the same immune response that follows transplantation of normal tissues, including antibody production and induction of sensitized T lymphocytes (the effectors of T-cell mediated immunity). Immunization requires exposing the recipient to small sublethal doses of tumor or to excision of a growing tumor. Tumors from other strains of animals (allogeneic) may be used for immunization, provided tumors are available in both strains with the same tumor-specific antigen, eg, in the virus-induced tumors. Because of the presence of foreign normal tissue antigens, such allogeneic tumors induce immunity against the common tumor antigen even as they are being rejected by the host.

If the host has had previous contact with a specific virus responsible for the tumor, tumors may not develop. This implies that the virus has caused some cells to be partially transformed or, at least, to produce the new tumor-specific antigen without evidence of a growing tumor. This same phenomenon is seen in vitro when normal cells exposed to a tumor-inducing virus develop tumor-specific transplantation antigen before they show any of the morphologic signs associated with malignant transformation. The immune response against the tumor can be adoptively transferred to nonimmune animals by sensitized lymphoid cells; only under special circumstances can this be accomplished by circulating antibody.

Antibody

Antibody induced by the growth of an antigenic tumor can be detected after its absorption to tumor cells by using fluorescent antibody, isotope-labeled antibody, immune adherence, complement fixation, or death of the tumor cells in the presence of complement. Cytolysis is rarely seen unless the tumor is of lymphoid origin. Sensitivity to cytotoxic antibody is a property of lymphoid cells themselves, not of the malignancy. In fact, both normal and malignant lymphoid cells are lysed by appropriate antisera, but normal fibroblasts, sarcoma cells, epitheliel cells, and carcinomas are unaffected. Apparently, the density of antigenic sites on the surface of lymphoid cells allows them to bind both antibody and all the components of complement needed for cell lysis. Other cell types that have a sparse distribution of antigenic sites can bind antibody but are unable to react with all components of the complement system. Of course, factors such as the ability to repair cell membranes may also be involved.

Cellular Immunity

T lymphocytes are primarily responsible for tissue rejection in transplantation and the reaction against antigenic tumors. Upon exposure to antigenic cells in vivo or in vitro, or both, cytotoxic cells are induced and multiply. This process requires a few days for primary immunization but less time for subsequent restimulation. In the cytotoxic process, a short recognition period is followed by a few minutes of actual contact, during which the cytotoxic lymphocytes fatally injure the target cells. If they are then separated, the cytotoxic cell is capable of repeating the process with more target cells. The nature of the fatal injury is not known, but the complete killing process requires less than an hour to complete.

T-cell cytotoxicity has been studied extensively in allogeneic systems, where it is directed against normal transplantation antigens. In experimental animal systems, cytotoxicity has been convincingly demonstrated against syngeneic tumors induced by viruses but not in tumors induced by chemical carcinogen. More importantly, T-cell cytotoxicity has not been easy to demonstrate in vitro against human tumors. T-cell mediated cytotoxicity, which can be demonstrated in short-term cultures, should be distinguished from cytotoxicity by other cell types that lead to target-cell destruction or to inhibition of tumor-cell growth in vitro, but such cultures may require from 24 to 48 hours. This latter cytotoxicity may be mediated by a variety of cells, including cytotoxic T cells, macrophages, killer cells, or natural killer cells, all of which require up to two days to act. Forty-eight hours is, of course, sufficient time for *new* cytotoxic cells to generate or for memory cells to be stimulated. With time, this increase in cytotoxicity may be responsible for the high levels of background or nonspecific cytotoxicity that have been observed frequently with control lymphocytes from normal, nonimmunized (ie, nontumorbearing) individuals in 24- to 48-hour assays.

In another form of cellular cytotoxicity, antibody-dependent cellular cytotoxicity (ADCC) or lymphocyte-dependent antibody (LDA), cytotoxic lymphocytes are attached to target cells by antibody – the antigen-specific portion binding to the target and the Fc portion binding to the lymphocyte. It is not clear whether the cell, termed a killer cell (K cell) and responsible for ADCC or LDA, originates from a T cell, B cell, or macrophage.

Many other immunologic phenomena, which may or may not be related to T-cell mediated cytotoxicity, are included under the general heading of Cellular Immunity. These phenomena include: "natural killer" (NK) cells, which may represent the natural defense counterpart to acquired immunity; lymphocyte stimulation, which usually precedes or is associated with the development of significant numbers of cytotoxic cells; and macrophage migration inhibition, which reflects some aspect of T-cell stimulation with the release of a soluble mediator. All of these, including T-cell cytotoxicity, are in vitro expressions of immune activity. Their relationship to each other and to what takes place in vivo still has to be determined. However, because tumors showing signs of rejection are often infiltrated with lymphoid cells, it is assumed that under optimal circumstances some forms of cellular immunity, including cytotoxicity, may take place in vivo.

Animals that have had no previous exposure to antigenic tumors still exhibit some resistance to low-dose challenges of tumor cells. This resistance can be greatly reduced by irradiation or significantly increased by viral infection. It is mediated by lymphoid cells that are neither T cells, B cells, nor macrophages. Although most pronounced in infants or young animals, resistance decreases markedly in adults but can be revived by a variety of measures, most notably acute viral infection. This natural resistance is relatively nonspecific and is not increased by immune stimulation. Considerable attention is now being given to NK cells as possible mediators of immune surveillance against cancer in normal individuals. Their in vivo role is not clear, and their interactions with other components of the immune system are only now being examined.

The Integrated Immune Response

It is now known that the immune response involves many interacting cell types. Some of the recognized cell populations and their functions are diagramed in Figure 79, but the total extent of these interactions is not yet known. The major compartments are the B (bone-marrow-derived) lymphocytes, which evolve into antibody-producing plasma cells, and the T (thymus-derived) lymphocytes, which evolve into effector cells of cell-mediated immunity. This latter group, already known to be quite complex, includes several subpopulations such as cytotoxic cells, helper T cells, and suppressor cells – all with highly specialized functions. Among these functions are the capacities to interact with antigen, antigenic cells, macrophages, B cells, and other subpopulations of T cells. In addition to interacting with B cells for antibody production, helper T cells release a variety of soluble factors that work at a

distance. These include macrophage inhibition factor, macrophage activation factor, lymphokines, blastogenic factor, and the inflammatory factors associated with delayed hypersensitivity (see chapters 4 and 5).

In addition, the immune system has self-regulating mechanisms that include mechanisms for shutting itself off. Subpopulations of T cells, macrophages, and B cells are capable of suppressing cells in their own compartments as well as cells in other interacting compartments. This is accomplished directly by appropriate suppressor cells and indirectly by production of soluble suppressor factors. Again, most of these are in vitro observations, and their significance in vivo is not known.

Consideration of the integrated immune response forces us to look more closely at the range of specificities of the various tumor antigens. With the exception of the ubiquitous tumor-associated antigen CEA, the chemical structure is not known for any tumor-specific antigen. Moreover, the various components of the immune system may "see" an antigenic tumor through quite different eyes. Some antigens are recognized by antibody and B cells, some by cytotoxic T cells, and some by both. Antibody and B cells more easily recognize soluble antigens, whereas T cells more easily recognize cellular antigens. Cytotoxic T cells, however, have a complex recognition interaction with an antigenic target cell. To react to the tumor antigen, the T cell must *also* recognize the major histocompatibility antigens and must have some of the *same* self-antigens as the antagonist tumor cell. This requirement is not shared by antibody and B cells; so they have different specificities than T cells.

From our present knowledge of the interaction between tumor antigens and the immune system, we cannot describe the antigens recognized by T cells, B cells, or antibody. Different immunologic assays may detect entirely different tumor antigens on the same tumor cells. This creates uncertainty and even confusion in our attempts to unravel the specificity and biochemistry of these antigens. In particular, we lack critical information about the antigens that react with T cells. The chemical nature and relative importance of these antigens will probably not become clear until they can be solubilized and shown to react with T cells. Even then, the antigens may require processing by macrophages or presentation to the T cell in some special form.

Figure 79
Lymphocyte interactions in immunity

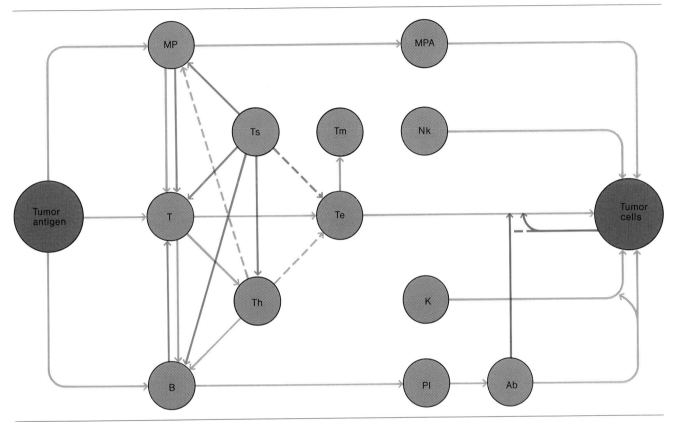

The network of interactions between various immune cells as they may be affected by an antigenic tumor suggests a high level of internal regulation. Green arrows represent activation of the immune response. Red arrows represent suppression.

T = T-cell
Ts = Suppressor T-cell
Te = Effector T-cell
Th = Helper T-cell
Tm = Memory cell
MP = Macrophage cell
MPA = Activated macrophage
B = B cell
Pl = Plasma cell
Ab = Antibody
K = Killer cell
NK = Natural killer cell

Figure 80
Worldwide distribution of Burkitt lymphoma

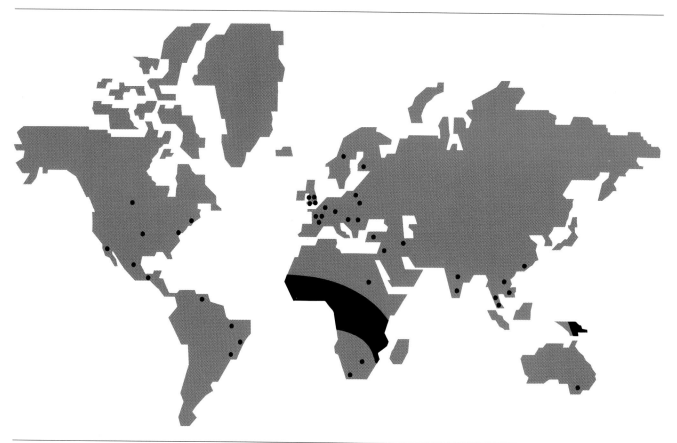

Areas in black are the only regions in which the tumor is known to be endemic. The western half of New Guinea is not shaded because of lack of data. Recent information suggests more cases in Brazil. Black dots indicate sporadic occurrences.

First discovered in 1957, the interferons are a group of low molecular weight glycoproteins that have a strong antiviral effect. They are produced by a variety of cell types in response to virus infection or by T cells, B cells, and macrophages following stimulation by antigens or mitogens. There is some evidence that they regulate the immune response by suppressing the production of antibody or cell-mediated immunity. NK cells, on the other hand, not only produce interferons but also appear to be stimulated by them.

In addition to their antiviral and possible immunoregulatory functions, the interferons are potent inhibitors of cell growth in many systems. They inhibit the growth of many normal and malignant cells in culture and inhibit the growth of some experimental tumors in vivo. Currently, the interferons are undergoing preliminary trials as antitumor agents in the treatment of human cancer.

Human Tumors

One of the most important questions in tumor immunology research today is whether immunology will have useful application to human malignancy. To date, the most convincing and stimulating studies involve the possible link between antigen specificity and etiology as established with experimental virus-induced tumors. Recent findings of common tumor-specific antigens, combined with virological studies, indicate that Burkitt lymphoma may be of viral origin. This was the first human tumor to be subjected to intensive immunologic study. The fact that this tumor is largely confined to the humid, tropical portions of Central Africa (Figure 80) suggested an arthropod vector and possible infectious etiology. More importantly, it was found that (1) the tumor could be cured by chemotherapy in a significant number of patients (Figure 81) and (2) several spontaneous remissions and cures occurred in the absence of any therapy.

Figure 81
Treatment of Burkitt lymphoma

a

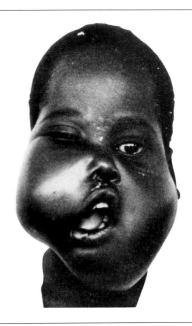

b

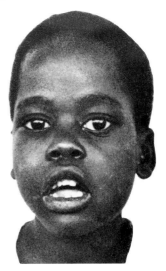

(a) Six-year-old boy with Burkitt lymphoma of the right maxilla, left mandible, and left submandibular salivary gland. (b) Marked tumor regression after treatment with irradiated tumor cell vaccine and orthomerphalan. Child is now classified as a long-term survivor.

In the serum of patients with Burkitt lymphoma, specific circulating antibody against their own tumor cells was detected by immunofluorescence. With one exception – nasopharyngeal carcinoma found in the Far East – sera from Burkitt lymphoma patients rarely reacted with tumor cells from patients who had other types of tumors or with normal controls. Likewise, sera from other tumor-bearing patients and from normal controls rarely reacted with Burkitt cells. These findings suggest that Burkitt lymphoma is antigenic to its host and that it causes the production of antibody that is adsorbed to the surface of the tumor cell. In addition, cells from one Burkitt patient share common antigens with those from other Burkitt patients. This fact is reminiscent of the experimental findings for virus-induced tumors. A herpes-like viral particle (Epstein-Barr virus, EBV) has been recovered from Burkitt cells (Figures 82, 83, 84). Isolation of a virus particle from cultured tumor cells, however, does not constitute proof that the virus is directly responsible for the malignancy. The uptake by cultured cells of passenger viruses from the environment is all too frequent.

Although nasopharyngeal carcinoma (one of the most common cancers in the Orient) is a morphologically different tumor and has its own peculiar geographic pattern, virological and immunologic studies suggest that this tumor is also related to EBV. The virus particles recovered from Burkitt lymphoma and from nasopharyngeal carcinoma are antigenically very similar to the virus associated with the common disease infectious mononucleosis. Whether these are the same virus particles that cause different clinical diseases under different circumstances or whether they are different viruses that "wear similar clothes" is unclear.

Why Do Tumors Succeed?

Although we know that many tumors are antigenic and can induce an immune response, we do not know how frequently the immune systems of healthy individuals encounter and destroy aberrant cells. If the normal immune response is capable of preventing or inhibiting tumor growth, the tumor may take three routes to ensure its success: take advantage of lapses in immune capacity, escape from immune control, and suppress the immune response. Currently, it is not known if *any* of these proposed mechanisms play a significant role in human cancer.

Lapses in Immune Capacity

Studies of the immune capacity (particularly cellular immunity) in normal individuals reveal occasions when the immune capacity is significantly depressed. This is most frequently associated with viral infections, including the common cold. Other stressful situations, including general anesthesia and surgery, are associated with immune depression. Many of these lapses are unavoidable, and most are transient. However, they suggest that the potential tumor may have occasional opportunities to become established.

Figure 82
Empty EBV capsid

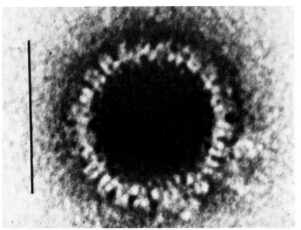

Composite views of EBV cultured from patients with lymphoma, leukemias, or infectious mononucleosis. Negative stain of empty viral capsid.

Figure 83
Capsids of EBV

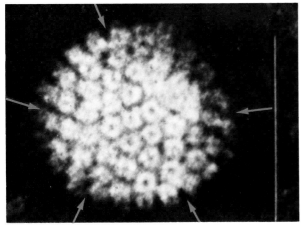

Negative stain of extracellular virions showing surface subunits (capsomeres – 162).

Figure 84
DNA within EBV

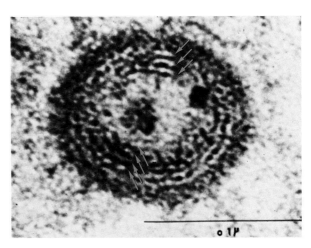

Positive stain of intracellular virions. Arrows indicate deoxyribonucleic acid (DNA) coils within capsid. Reference line = 1,000 angstrom units.

123

Age: Although difficult to measure quantitatively, it is likely that the general human immune capacity rises rapidly in infancy, maintains a plateau throughout most of adult life, and gradually declines in later years. Superimposed on this is the incidence of malignancy – relatively low in youth but increasing dramatically in later life. Experimental studies raise the possibility that infection with a tumor-inducing virus may occur in utero during the immunologically incompetent period. The virus may then lie dormant for years before manifesting itself late in adult life.

Immunologic deficiency diseases: Among the fates befalling children with immunologic deficiency diseases is a markedly increased likelihood of malignancy – particularly of the reticuloendothelial system (Table 23). In children with the acquired type of hypogammaglobulinemia, ataxia telangiectasia, and the Wiscott-Aldrich syndrome, the incidence of leukemia, lymphoma, and reticulum cell sarcoma is far higher than in normal children of the same age.

Model systems for the development of immunologic defects have utilized thymectomy and irradiation. Such nonspecific inhibition of the immune response generally results in a higher incidence of tumors, with a shorter time lapse between contact with the inducing agent and appearance of the tumor and with more rapid tumor growth. Conversely, some experimental virus tumors of the reticuloendothelial system appear to originate in thymic tissue and are prevented by early thymectomy.

Immunosuppression: Use of immunosuppressive agents to facilitate organ transplantation in humans also results in nonspecific suppression of the immune response. These patients have a significantly increased incidence of malignancy – about one percent of all transplant patients. Although the proportion of tumors of the reticuloendothelial system is somewhat higher than expected, the spectrum of tumors encountered in these patients is much broader than those found in patients with immunologic deficiency diseases.

Table 23
Incidence of primary malignancy in immunologic deficiency diseases and renal transplant patients

Disease	Incidence of malignancy	Type of malignancy
Sex-linked agamma-globulinemia* (Brutons)	5% (10,000 x normal)	Acute lymphatic leukemia
III-IV Pharyngeal pouch syndrome (DiGeorge)	–	–
Severe combined immunodeficiency	5%	Lymphoreticular
Wiskott-Aldrich	10%	Lymphoreticular
Common variable immunodeficiency	10%	Lymphoreticular and carcinomas
Isolated IgA	?	Adenocarcinoma of stomach (1 case)
Ataxia telangiectasia	10%	Lymphoreticular, sarcoma, carcinoma
Renal transplant patients**	1.26% (190/15,000) (25 x normal)	Epithelial (62%) Mesenchymal (38%)

*From Richard A. Gatti and Robert A. Good
**From Olga Jonasson and Israel Penn and Thomas E. Starzl

Escape From Immune Control

Natural selection in the tumor: Until recently it was widely believed that most tumors are antigenic. It now appears that this is probably not true. Most experimental virus-induced tumors and some chemical-induced tumors are antigenic, but most spontaneous tumors in animals and in humans are not. Moreover, those tumors that are antigenic present relatively weak antigens compared to the strong normal transplantation antigens. This suggests that weakly antigenic or nonantigenic tumors may grow *because* of their poor immunogenicity, whereas strongly antigenic tumors succumb to immune surveillance. Even among premalignant cells that will require one or two more steps to become fully malignant or within the microscopic tumor struggling for survival, selection for lesser antigenicity may be important. Far from being a uniform group of cells, the growing tumor is heterogenous, and the genetic controls have been relaxed considerably, allowing new cell variants to appear in every succeeding generation. Against this population variation, the immune system applies constant pressure. The host may apply immunologic pressure against the cells that are most antigenic and spare those tumor cells that are less antigenic, thus permitting a tumor to grow whose immunogenicity is acceptably low or nonexistent.

Natural selection in the host: Virus-induced tumors are not uniformly immunogenic. Although all oncogenic viruses produce new viral and tumor-specific cellular antigens, there is often a wide discrepancy between the distribution of the virus and the development of actual tumors in the natural hosts. Paradoxically, the *more* widespread a tumor virus is in its own species in nature, the *less* likely it is to cause tumors in its native host (eg, polyoma virus of the mouse, or EBV of humans). However, the same virus may be highly oncogenic in a different host species. Apparently, the native host accepts the virus but protects itself against tumor induction much better than does the foreign host. It has been suggested that evolutionary selection results in the resistance of natural hosts to the oncogenic effects of some ancient tumor-inducing viruses, presumably by immunologic rejection of antigenic premalignant cells. Other oncogenic viruses that are less widespread in nature (eg, feline leukemia and Marek disease of chickens) often affect their hosts at epidemic rates *and* frequently produce more fatal tumors in their natural hosts. Increased infectivity and virulence of the virus or inability of the host to select or evolve effective resistance to the antigens of either the virus or the tumor may be responsible for this.

Suppression of the Immune Response by the Tumor

Besides escaping from immunologic detection, tumors can also fight back against an immune attack.

Tumor size and the effect of tumor dose: Unlike the immune response to normal tissues, which is almost an all-or-none phenomenon, the specific immune response to tumors has very real limits. A highly immunized animal may be quite resistant to challenge with a moderate number of tumor cells when compared to untreated controls. However, if the number of challenging tumor cells is sufficiently large, the cells usually overcome this resistance and develop into fatal malignancies. This may represent some nonspecific conditioning of the host environment by the tumor. It may also represent specific immunologic protection offered by the release of tumor antigen or by the aggregation of large numbers of cells. Similar findings are seen in experimental animals challenged with small inocula of tumors while a large primary tumor is growing. Under these conditions, secondary challenges often will not grow, although the initial tumor grows relentlessly. This may explain why metastases in experimental and clinical tumors are relatively rare considering the number of potentially metastatic cells that can be found in the bloodstream.

Enhancement and blocking: It has been shown with a variety of experimental tumors, primarily sarcomas and carcinomas, that a transplanted tumor may grow better in vivo in the presence of serum from an immune or tumor-bearing donor. It appears that the serum contains a factor(s) that protects the tumor cell against otherwise cytotoxic effector cells. Transplantation studies showed that antibody provided this protection or enhancement. In vivo, serum from the tumor-bearing animal can be shown to interfere with cellular cytotoxicity. In most of these studies, enhancement and blocking have been attributed to inhibition of cytotoxic T cells, NK cells, or K cells, although the effector cell has not been identified. In addition, antibody, antigen, and even complexes of antibody plus antigen have all been implicated in this process (Figure 85). It is not known whether blocking or enhancement are important factors or if they have any role in the growth of human cancers.

Tolerance: Blocking and inhibition of the existing immune response are peripheral phenomena, whereas tolerance implies central inhibition by overwhelming the immune system with antigen; thus few, if any, immune cells and antibodies are produced. In the presence of weak transplantation antigens, central tolerance can be induced by exposing adult animals to large amounts of antigen for short periods or by prolonged exposure to small amounts of antigen. This latter procedure approximates what happens when a small tumor escapes immune destruction, survives for a long time, and releases small amounts of antigen until specific tolerance is induced. The occurrence of metastatic carcinoma of the breast 15 to 20 years after the removal of the primary tumor may be due to slow development of tolerance.

Nonspecific inhibition of immune capacity: As outlined here, enhancement and tolerance are mechanisms by which a growing tumor may suppress a specific immune response directed against it. It is more difficult to explain the frequent finding that the overall immune capacity of some tumor-bearing individuals is significantly reduced. This is seen with a variety of tumors at all stages.

Figure 85
Immune surveillance and escape

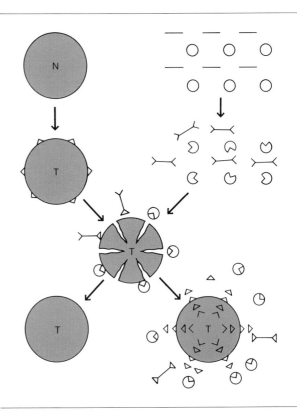

It is postulated that the antigens acquired by the normal cell on becoming malignant activate an immune surveillance system. To escape from this, the tumor may revert to a nonantigenic form or may shed large amounts of antigen into the circulation and block the immune response.

Reduced immune capacity can be detected by a variety of techniques: reduced numbers of lymphocytes, reduced responsiveness of lymphocytes to stimulation by specific antigens or nonspecific lymphokines, and impaired cutaneous hypersensitivity to new or recall antigens. The relationship of this immunologic impairment to tumor growth is not clear, although several studies have indicated that impaired immune capacity is associated with poor prognosis. However, these are statistical studies with numerous exceptions, and many of them have not been confirmed. With the exception of patients with leukemia or those receiving high doses of cytotoxic drugs or radiation, most cancer patients are *not* immunologic cripples and are *not* unusually susceptible to bizarre viral, bacterial, or fungal infections.

Numerous attempts have failed to demonstrate a potent suppressor of immune capacity that is produced directly by tumors. With increasing understanding of its many feedback controls, we may find that the immune system shuts itself off at a central and nonspecific level.

Immunotherapy

Immunization against a tumor may be prophylactic (against a tumor that the individual has yet to encounter) or therapeutic (against one that is already growing progressively).

Prophylactic immunization: Prophylaxis is one goal of immunotherapy. Experimental models have demonstrated that immunity can be established against either the causative agent or the tumor-specific antigens of the neoplastic cells. Oncogenic viruses are useful because they are potentially accessible, antigenic, and may be subject to manipulations of infectivity and pathogenicity. Because infection of a cell by oncogenic virus alters cellular antigens, immunization against these altered cellular antigens may provide protection even when the virus itself cannot be influenced immunologically. Both of these approaches must await the isolation of proven human oncogenic viruses and methods for detecting populations at high risk from them.

Nonspecific immunologic stimulation: Several microbiological agents that include *Bacille Calmette Guerin* (BCG), *Corynebacterium parvum*, and *Bordetella pertussis* are capable of general stimulation of the lymphoreticular system. In experimental models, these agents inhibit the development of spontaneous tumors, the induction of tumors by chemicals and viruses, and the growth of transplantable tumors. They can also cause rejection of small established transplantable tumors. Stimulation with BCG appears to affect both cell-mediated immunity and antibody production, although the mechanism of this stimulation and its effect on tumor growth are not known.

Active immunization against tumor-specific antigens: Augmentation or modification of the tumor-specific immune response by immunization with tumor cells or cell-free antigen preparations is the basis of active immunotherapy against a specific tumor. The use of autologous tumor cells that are rendered incapable of growth by irradiation or treatment with mitomycin C represents the simplest form of specific active immunotherapy. This approach assumes that inoculations of cells at many sites will activate a larger portion of the overall immune capacity than does the original tumor growing in situ. Killed or inactivated allogeneic tumor cells may be inoculated if they share the same common tumor-specific antigens as those of the tumor being treated. The surface of the tumor cells can also be modified to make them more immunogenic.

Specific active immunotherapy may use soluble tumor antigen extracts prepared from tumors obtained at surgery or at autopsy. Some tumor antigens can be recovered, concentrated, or stored without loss of antigenicity. However, when inducing specific immunization with intact tumor cells or with cell-free soluble antigen extract, the nature of the antigen, the form in which it is presented, and the route of administration may all be very important. Unfortunately, soluble antigens released by tumors in vivo may block an effective immune response – a possible undesirable result of injecting exogenous antigenic material. A final approach to specific active immunization is to stimulate host lymphocytes with tumor cells (or antigen) by cultivating them together in vitro.

Adoptive transfer of immunity: An entirely different approach to immunotherapy is to transfer the machinery for continuous production of specific immunity from one individual to another, rather than to transfer a product of the immune response. Initially, such transfer was attempted by exchanging lymphoid cells between two individuals bearing similar tumors. Frequently, the patients were previously immunized against each other's tumor to increase the likelihood of obtaining highly sensitized lymphocytes. The drawback to this approach is that the lymphocytes are foreign to the recipient and will undergo prompt rejection, probably before they have any chance to interact with the tumor. However, the allogeneic lymphoid cells may contain immunologic information that can be transferred to a recipient's lymphoid cells, better equipping them to deal with the tumor. Packets of information, such as transfer factor and immune RNA, have been transferred to recipients, but evidence of specific immunologic stimulation is unconvincing.

Immunotherapy of Human Cancer

Attempts to control human cancer by immunotherapy have not lived up to the hopes created by the first optimistic reports of a few years ago. Results of some of the larger and more optimistic studies were questioned because they could not be repeated, and eventually they were judged invalid because the studies were poorly designed and controlled. These studies include nonspecific immunization (particularly with BCG), specific immunization with syngeneic or allogeneic tumor cells, and transfer of immunity with lymphoid cells or their products. A few studies with concurrent, randomized controls yielded positive results, and these, together with numerous anecdotes, suggest that immunotherapy has helped some patients and should receive further study. Presently, however, there is no tumor for which any existing form of immunotherapy should be considered routine, and there are few instances where it is advisable except on a well-planned study basis.

Prospectus

The disappointing results of clinical trials with immunotherapy have eroded two of our most cherished beliefs: that all tumors are antigenic and that cancer patients are immunologically deficient and need only be stimulated properly to overcome their tumors. It now appears more likely that immunodeficiency is triggered by the malignancy rather than the other way around. Better understanding of the mechanism of the immunosuppression often seen in malignancy may enable us to overcome it. Similarly, the tumor that is not immunogenic is not necessarily beyond the reach of the immune system. Several studies have shown that it may be possible to add new antigens to tumor cells to make them immunogenic. Antigenic modification of the tumor cell can be accomplished in experimental systems by coupling strongly antigenic haptens to the cell surface, by inducing production of new antigens with viruses or virus-derived information, or by hybridizing tumor cells with highly antigenic normal cells.

Currently, interaction between the immune response of the tumor-bearing individual and his malignancy is undergoing intense investigation. This has already provided a great deal of information about the etiology and biology of many tumors. However, the major goals of earlier diagnosis and effective immunization as a new mode of therapy continue to elude us. Presently, areas of particular interest include the internal regulatory balances of the immune system and methods for modulating these by outside influences. Although it is not likely that these goals will be achieved easily, they are being brought significantly closer by the dramatic expansion of our understanding of the immune system.

Immunosuppression

Introduction

Immunosuppressive therapy has developed as an empirical art in the pressurized atmosphere of clinical practice. In spite of (or perhaps because of) this, numerous advances that knowledgeable scientists once considered improbable have been achieved. Organ transplantation, as one example, was once an impractical dream. The results of kidney transplantation in the treatment of end-stage renal disease reflect the extraordinary progress in this field; under certain circumstances, the effectiveness of this procedure now exceeds that of chronic hemodialysis. There are also new ways of treating a variety of immunologic diseases. Nevertheless, there is still much to be learned about immunosuppression at both the fundamental and clinical levels.

Modification of the Immune Response

Antigen: Elimination of antigen, without which there is no immunity, cannot be overemphasized as a therapeutic maneuver within the grasp of every physician. Confronted with an immunologic disorder, the physician should at once ask two questions: What was the inciting antigen? How can I eliminate it? Naturally, removal of antigen from the patient (or the patient from the antigen) is not always feasible. Other means of nullifying immunogenicity of antigen remain, such as to prevent its contact with immunocompetent cells. For instance, foreign tissues transplanted into the anterior chamber of the eye survive because lymphocytes normally do not enter that structure. This principle underlies the success of corneal transplants, which are not rejected unless lymphatics invade the zone of implantation.

Antibody: Another way of nullifying immunogenicity is by administration of antibody. Presumably, the antibody combines with or coats antigenic sites, thus preventing their contact with immunocompetent cells. Desensitization therapy involves this principle by eliciting the synthesis of IgG antibodies that block interactions between the allergen and tissue-fixed IgE. Another example is the prevention of Rh sensitization. Anti-Rh antibodies obtained from human volunteers are administered to the mother at the time of highest risk of sensitization, thereby nullifying the immunogenicity of the infant's Rh-positive cells in the Rh-negative mother. The procedure is virtually 100% effective and has been highly successful in the elimination of erythroblastosis fetalis as a clinical problem (Figure 86).

Inhibition of Immunocompetent Cells

Attrition maneuvers: Either neonatal thymectomy or thoracic-duct drainage depletes the body of thymus-dependent lymphocytes. The former procedure removes the organ required for the maturation of T cells, whereas the latter works because the thoracic duct is one of the main routes taken by T cells in their circulation throughout the body. Both neonatal thymectomy and thoracic-duct drainage lead to severely impaired cell-mediated immunity and inhibition of antibody synthesis, both of which depend on T cells.

Lymphocytolysis: Lymphocytes are the most radiation-sensitive cells of the body. Lymphocytes are also susceptible to corticosteroids, but the lymphocytes of some species are relatively resistant to these hormones. For example, the lymphocytes of both mice and rats are extremely sensitive to corticosteroids, whereas those of human beings are relatively resistant. The clinical effects of corticosteroids may be due primarily to inhibition of inflammatory responses. This effect may be caused by impaired traffic of inflammatory cells into sites of antigen deposition. Moreover, phagocytosis of antibody-coated cells is inhibited. In those species with radiation- and corticosteroid-sensitive lymphocytes, maximum immunosuppression occurs when these agents are given immediately before the antigenic challenge. If thymectomy and x-irradiation are combined, mature animals can be very effectively depleted of T cells because the x-rays destroy peripheral lymphocytes and the thymectomy prevents their repopulation from the central pool. Under these conditions, thymus-independent B cells from the marrow reseed lymph nodes and spleen. The result in an animal whose immunologic repertoire is virtually restricted to the functions of B cells (Figure 87).

Figure 86
Immunoprevention of hemolytic disease of the newborn (erythroblastosis fetalis)

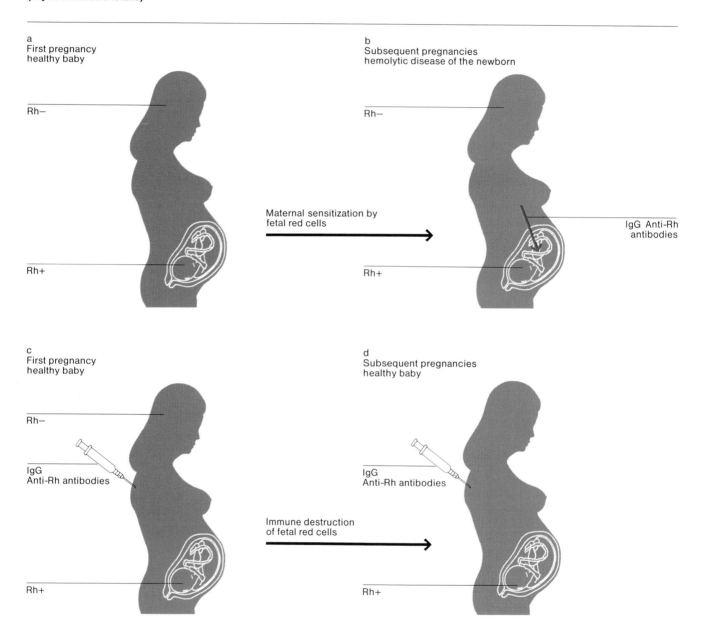

a
First pregnancy
healthy baby

Rh−

Rh+

Maternal sensitization by
fetal red cells

b
Subsequent pregnancies
hemolytic disease of the newborn

Rh−

Rh+

IgG Anti-Rh
antibodies

c
First pregnancy
healthy baby

Rh−

IgG
Anti-Rh antibodies

Rh+

Immune destruction
of fetal red cells

d
Subsequent pregnancies
healthy baby

Rh−

IgG
Anti-Rh antibodies

Rh+

During a pregnancy in which the mother is Rh− and the fetus Rh+, fetal red cells sensitize the mother, who produces anti-Rh antibodies (panel a). The maximum risk of sensitization occurs during the delivery of the baby, when large numbers of the infant's red cells escape through the placenta into the mother's blood. Therefore, first pregnancies are not usually harmful to the infant. During subsequent pregnancies, maternal IgG anti-Rh antibodies cross the placenta and lead to the destruction of the infant's Rh+ red cells. Severe hemolytic anemia of the newborn child or intrauterine death can result (panel b). Administration of anti-Rh antibodies prevents sensitization of the

mother by destruction of Rh+ fetal red cells that enter the maternal circulation (panel c). The antiserum, produced by human volunteers, is administered shortly after delivery of the baby (the time of maximum risk of sensitization). The maternal red cells are Rh− and are unaffected by the anti-Rh serum. Destruction of the Rh+ red cells (or the coating of their antigenic sites) by the antibody blocks maternal sensitization. The antibody must be administered after delivery or termination of all subsequent pregnancies in order to prevent isoimmunization of the mother (panel d).

Figure 87
Preparation of a "B" mouse

a. Thymectomy

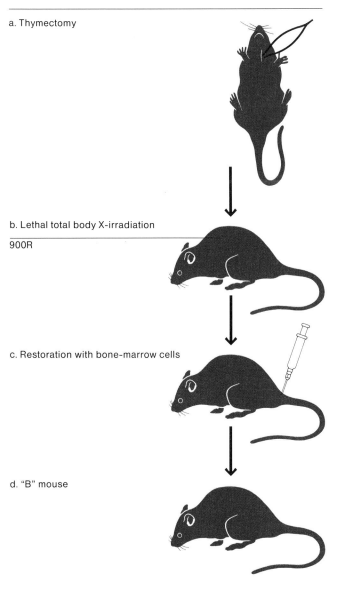

b. Lethal total body X-irradiation

900R

c. Restoration with bone-marrow cells

d. "B" mouse

This procedure selectively destroys all thymus-dependent lymphocytes. The first step, thymectomy (panel a), removes the organ that is required for the differentiation of bone marrow precursor cells (prothymocytes) into T lymphocytes. Thymectomy eliminates short-lived T cells but does not affect long-lived T cells. The latter cells are eliminated by lethal total body irradiation (panel b). The x-rays, however, also destroy most other lymphocytes as well as hematopoietic cells. Therefore, the irradiated mouse must be "restored" with bone marrow, which contains precursors to B cells as well as hematopoietic cells (panel c). Before inoculation, the marrow cells are treated with an antiserum (anti-theta) to destroy any T cells that may be present. Any prothymocytes in the inoculum cannot differentiate because of the lack of a thymus. As a further measure to eliminate remaining T lymphocytes, the restored mice are usually given one or more injections of antithymocyte serum. The final result is a mouse lacking detectable T lymphocytes (panel d).

Antilymphocyte serum (ALS): ALS was first studied by Metchnikoff at the turn of the 20th century, and more than 20 years ago its ability to depress cell-mediated immunity was discovered. ALS is prepared by immunization of one species with the lymphocytes (obtained from thymus, spleen, lymph nodes, or thoracic duct) of another (Figure 88). Horse and rabbit antihuman lymphocyte sera are currently employed in clinical studies. There are two important problems associated with these heterologous sera. The first is standardization; there is no reliable way of knowing the immunosuppressive potency of a given preparation because there is imperfect correlation between in vitro effects, such as agglutination of lymphocytes, and in vivo properties. Another problem is the immunogenicity of heterologous antilymphocyte serum, because the serum is a foreign protein and can cause serum sickness and allergic reactions. Antibodies elicited by the foreign protein result in a decreased therapeutic effectiveness of the ALS because the immunogenic material is rapidly cleared from the blood. It is sometimes difficult to know whether patients chronically treated with ALS actually benefit from its use; therefore, present clinical practice limits treatment to several weeks.

There is excellent evidence that ALS leads to the destruction of circulating lymphocytes. Lymphocytes coated with ALS probably behave like antibody-coated erythrocytes and are rapidly cleared from the blood by reticuloendothelial cells in the liver and spleen. Since ALS distributes itself preferentially in blood and lymph, the circulating lymphocytes (mainly T cells) are preferentially attacked. The most important immunological effect of ALS is, therefore, impaired cellular immunity. Immunosuppressive effects of ALS can be augmented in thymectomized animals by the mechanism previously described for x-ray treatment. The great power of ALS to inhibit cellular immunity accounts for its striking ability to retard the rejection of foreign tissues. However, the effect is not antigen-specific. Therefore, patients treated with ALS are highly susceptible to viral, fungal, and certain bacterial infections.

During the past several years, it has become apparent that some functional subsets of T cells can be distinguished by antisera. In the mouse, alloantisera have been prepared against T cells with either helper, suppressor, or cytotoxic functions. Also, naturally occurring autoantibodies against helper and suppressor T cells have been identified in human sera. Recently, it has been possible to prepare antibodies against functional subsets of human lymphocytes by immunization of other species. These antibodies may have certain therapeutic advantages over the relatively nonspecific antilymphocyte serum preparations that are currently available. There is, for example, evidence that certain immunodeficiency disorders, as well as some autoimmune diseases, may be caused by an imbalance between helper and suppressor T cells. The administration of antiserum directed against one or another of these subsets may restore the balance to normal.

Chemical Immunosuppression

Although cytotoxic drugs (Figure 89) can kill unstimulated lymphocytes, their major immunologic effects are focused on cells stimulated by antigen to undergo proliferation and differentiation. Generally, these drugs are less effective on cells that are already producing antibodies. The cells most susceptible to these agents are the dividing antigen-stimulated blasts that have not yet begun to secrete antibody. Thus, in experimental systems, the timing of drug administration is critical.

Alkylating agents: DNA is the main target of alkylating drugs. The nitrogen atoms of the purine and pyrimidine bases of DNA react with the alkylating agent and thereby weaken the structure of the double helix. Another effect of alkylation is the formation of rigid links between the two chains of the helix; these new bonds block DNA replication, and mitosis stops. Cyclophosphamide is an example of a powerful and clinically useful alkylating agent. This drug is inactive until phosphatases split the phosphoramide ring from the parent compound, thereby converting the prodrug into a highly active alkyl form.

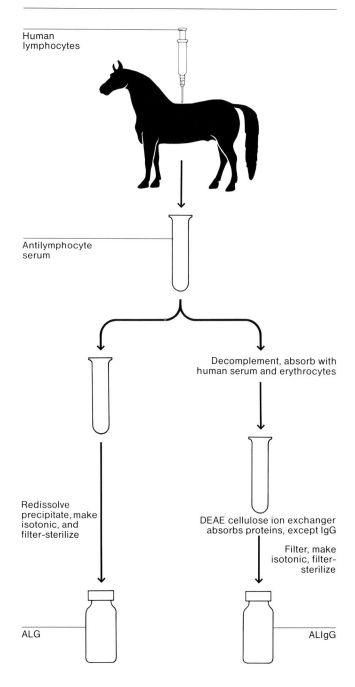

Figure 88
Schematic diagram for production of heterologous antilymphocyte antibody

Human lymphocytes

Antilymphocyte serum

Decomplement, absorb with human serum and erythrocytes

Redissolve precipitate, make isotonic, and filter-sterilize

DEAE cellulose ion exchanger absorbs proteins, except IgG

Filter, make isotonic, filter-sterilize

ALG

ALIgG

Cyclophosphamide

6-mercaptopurine

Azathioprine

Amethopterin (methotrexate)

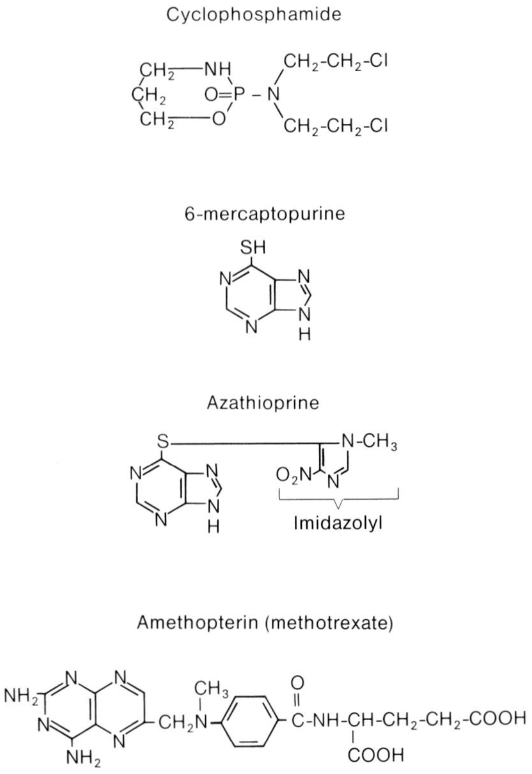

Alkylating agents affect many cells besides lymphocytes. These drugs are mutagenic, and there is increasing evidence that the chronic administration of alkylating agents is associated with an increased risk of malignancy. This complication is particularly striking when alkylating agents are used in combination with radiotherapy, as in the treatment of certain neoplastic diseases. Acute myelogenous leukemia has developed in 2% to 5% of patients with Hodgkin disease who received such combined therapy. Acute myelogenous leukemia has also occurred in patients who had either multiple myeloma or ovarian cancer and were aggressively treated with alkylating agents alone. There are also reports that some patients treated with alkylating agents for nonmalignant diseases, such as glomerulonephritis, developed acute myelogenous leukemia. Therefore, cyclophosphamide, chlorambucil, nitrogen mustard, and related compounds should be used with caution as immunosuppressive agents.

Purine antagonists: The prototype of this class of antimetabolite is 6-mercatopurine (6-MP), which impairs the early steps in purine biosynthesis as well as the utilization of inosinic acid. Normally, purine ribonucleotides inhibit the enzyme phosphoribosylpyrophosphate amidotransferase, which is essential for the first step in purine synthesis. The prototype 6-MP is converted to a purine ribonucleotide, and this fraudulent nucleotide causes feedback inhibition of purine biosynthesis. One of the products of 6-MP metabolism is thioinosinic acid. The naturally occurring counterpart of this compound is inosinic acid, the first purine of the biosynthetic pathway to be synthesized de novo. Thioinosinic acid, by substituting for inosinic acid, blocks the subsequent steps of purine synthesis. The cells affected by 6-MP thus perform a lethal synthesis by manufacturing substances able to disrupt their own biochemical processes.

A second purine analog of considerable importance, azathioprine, has an imidazole ring attached to the sulfur atom of 6-MP. Although there is no compelling evidence that azathioprine has decided advantages over 6-MP in humans, the former agent has largely replaced 6-MP as an immunosuppressive agent.

The development of cancer is a matter of concern in patients treated with purine antagonists as it is in those treated with alkylating agents. In recipients of renal transplants who have been treated with azathioprine and prednisone, the two most common neoplasms are skin cancers and a peculiar lymphoma that resembles immunoblastic sarcoma. An increased incidence of acute myelogenous leukemia, which occurs with alkylating agents, has not been associated with azathioprine therapy. The pathogenesis of neoplasms in azathioprine-treated patients is not clear. The drug is mutagenic, and the tendency toward the development of lymphomas may be due to this effect combined with impaired regulation of lymphocyte function.

Folic acid analogs: Folic acid, which is essential for DNA synthesis, is converted to its active form, tetrahydrofolate, by the enzyme dihydrofolate reductase. Tetrahydrofolate, in turn, converts deoxyuridylate to thymidylate – the latter is the rate-limiting nucleotide in DNA synthesis. Thus, any interruption in the supply of tetrahydrofolate will lead to a cessation of DNA synthesis. Methotrexate, a powerful folic acid analog, inhibits dihydrofolate reductase and so reduces DNA synthesis but has relatively little direct influence on RNA synthesis. Cells affected by this compound stop dividing but continue to synthesize RNA and proteins. One result of this differential action on nucleic acids is the development of the megaloblast.

Toxicology of chemical immunosuppressants: The biologic effects of cytotoxic drugs are a function of the administered dose. When large amounts are given, the secondary biochemical effects of these agents become evident, and toxicity ensues. In high doses, cytotoxic drugs kill slowly dividing lymphocytes, so the result is nonspecific immunosuppression. Other cells that are engaged in DNA synthesis are also damaged, eg, cells of the bone marrow and gastrointestinal tract, which are highly susceptible to these agents. Therefore, the major manifestations of toxicity of the chemical immunosuppressants are hypoplasia of the bone marrow and injury to the gastrointestinal tract. Alopecia, sterility, and hemorrhagic cystitis are toxic effects peculiar to cyclophosphamide, whereas methotrexate is hepatotoxic.

High doses of antimetabolites and alkylating agents kill T cells and B cells indiscriminately, although at lower doses, cyclophosphamide destroys antigen-reactive T cells preferentially. A corollary to this effect is that thymectomy can greatly increase the immunosuppressive effect of cyclophosphamide. Another interesting phenomenon is that rodent suppressor T cells are highly susceptible to cyclophosphamide. When, for example, mice are challenged with antigen and treated with relatively small amounts of the drug, they show an augmented immune response. This effect appears to be due to a relatively increased susceptibility of suppressor T cells to cyclophosphamide.

Nonspecific immunosuppression is the greatest stumbling block in immunosuppressive therapy, and often the physician must decide on a trade-off between the possible advantages of treatment and the disadvantages of immunologic crippling. Still, when prudently administered, immunosuppressive drugs can be relatively free of toxic effects. Nevertheless, physicians who administer these agents must be alert for complications. Interestingly, several experimental models showed that antigen-specific immunosuppression (immunologic tolerance) can be induced in animals treated with cytotoxic drugs. Presumably, the drug disrupts antigen-activated clones (Figure 90). However, an effect mediated by the action of these compounds on suppressor T cells has not been excluded. The differential effects of certain chemical compounds on functional subsets of lymphocytes, as indicated by the example of the effects of low doses of cyclophosphamide on suppressor T cells, suggest that compounds specific for certain classes of lymphocytes may be developed.

The macrophage is resistant to most cytotoxic agents, but x-irradiation may impair the cell's ability to break down phagocytosed substances (radiation-indigestion phenomenon). Recent evidence indicates that corticosteroids exert powerful effects on the macrophages of certain species, perhaps including humans. In addition to their inhibitory effects on lymphocytes, antilymphocyte serum and cytotoxic drugs may exert powerful anti-inflammatory effects by interfering with monocytes and macrophages. From the clinical point of view, inhibition of inflammation may be just as useful as immunosuppression.

Other Therapeutic Options

Plasmapheresis: Plasmapheresis, the replacement of large volumes of plasma by albumin, was suggested as a therapeutic maneuver more than 65 years ago. A technique that permits the removal of as much as four liters of plasma within two hours has now been developed. It has been successfully used in Waldenström macroglobulinemia, which is characterized by large amounts of IgM and hyperviscosity of the plasma. Plasmapheresis has been applied with increasing frequency for conditions in which the pathogenetic mechanism is caused by circulating soluble immune complexes (such as glomerulonephritis) or antibodies (Goodpasture syndrome or myasthenia gravis). Striking clinical improvements have been reported in myasthenia gravis, and the levels of antibodies to acetylcholine receptors have been reduced by as much as 20% of the pretreatment levels by plasmapheresis. Encouraging results have also been obtained in Goodpasture syndrome, in rapidly progressive glomerulonephritis, and in systemic lupus erythematosus. Plasmapheresis is a promising approach for patients with fulminant, life-threatening immunologic disturbances.

Solid-phase immunoadsorbents: Certain antigens or antibodies can be removed from plasma by passing it over an immunoadsorbent column to which has been bound the antibody (for removal of the corresponding antigen) or antigen (for the removal of the corresponding antibody). This interesting technic has been used to treat digitalis poisoning by extracorporeal circulation of the plasma over an immunoadsorbent column to which digitalis antibodies have been covalently bound. Antibodies to DNA can also be removed from the circulation of rabbits by passage of the plasma over an immunoadsorbent column made of DNA bound to

Figure 90
Drug-induced immunological tolerance

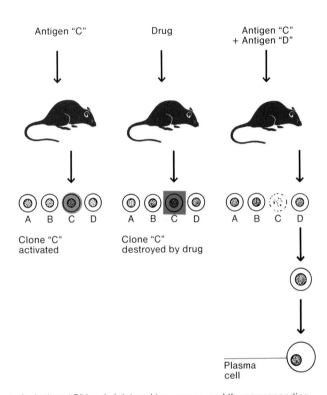

Left: Antigen "C" is administered to a mouse, and the corresponding clone of immune cells is activated. Center: The following day, a cytotoxic drug is given that destroys clone "C" because activated cells are more sensitive to the drug. Right: Several days later antigen "C" and a new antigen "D" are given to the animal. A normal immune response occurs toward antigen "D." However, no response occurs toward antigen "C" because the specific clone has been previously destroyed. The animal has been made specifically tolerant to "C."

cellulose. Similarly, circulating DNA has been extracted by extracorporeal circulation of plasma over a column of nylon microspheres to which deoxyribonuclease has been bound. This procedure also removes DNA and anti-DNA complexes from the plasma of experimental animals. The advantage of the immunoadsorbent column technic over plasmapheresis is that it specifically removes the pathogenetic agent, whereas the entire plasma volume must be replaced in plasmapheresis.

Vincristine: The vinca alkaloids, such as vincristine and vinblastine, bind to tubulin, which is the structural protein of microtubules. Although these agents are not particularly immunosuppressive, vincristine is effective by some unknown mechanism in patients with autoimmune thrombocytopenic purpura. Conceivably, the alkaloid binds to the tubulin of macrophages, thereby impairing the macrophage's ability to ingest antibody-coated platelets. This interpretation is supported by the interesting observation that the administration of platelets that had been treated with vinblastine in vitro led to improvement in severe cases of autoimmune thrombocytopenic purpura. Presumably, the vinblastine-loaded platelets were ingested by macrophages which were, in turn, specifically intoxicated by the drug that was bound to the administered platelets. Thus, the drug-treated platelet was a Trojan horse. There is considerable novelty in this approach, especially in cases of immune destruction of circulating blood cells.

Penicillamine: Penicillamine (β', β''-dimethylcysteine) is a metabolite of penicillin that has been used for years in the treatment of Wilson disease and in cysteinuria. Penicillamine, a thiol compound, can rupture the disulfide bridges that maintain the structure of IgM. Because rheumatoid factor is an IgM antibody, it was reasoned that, through this peripheral mechanism, penicillamine might benefit patients with rheumatoid arthritis. Several prospective, controlled clinical trials demonstrated the efficacy of penicillamine in the treatment of severe rheumatoid arthritis, but the development of thrombocytopenia, neutropenia, or proteinuria may limit its use. It is now believed that the original rationale for the use of penicillamine in rheumatoid arthritis is incorrect because rheumatoid factor levels decline only after clinical improvement occurs. Nevertheless, the chemical disruption of pathogenetic antibodies remains an intriguing possibility.

Levamisole: An alternative to the use of immunosuppression is to correct presumed imbalances in the immune system that may lead to the production of autoantibodies. One prominent theory of autoimmune disease postulates a deficiency in suppressor cells as the fundamental defect. This implies that *potentiation* of the immune response rather than *suppression* may be of clinical benefit in autoimmune disease. Levamisole is an antihelminthic drug with immunostimulatory properties in experimental animals; it also increases resistance to certain bacteria and viruses in laboratory animals. The drug has been tried in several immunologic diseases with interesting results, and it may be of benefit in the treatment of rheumatoid arthritis. It seems worthwhile to pursue possible therapeutic actions of other immunostimulants in autoimmune disease and to compare them with the actions of immunosuppressants.

Clinical Applications

Physicians must use their best clinical judgment when prescribing potent immunosuppressants. Regular blood tests, frequent physical examinations, and awareness of the danger of infection are mandatory. The previously mentioned increased incidence of cancer in patients treated with certain immunosuppressants is a risk factor that must be considered in making the therapeutic decision. Other long-term complications, such as ovarian failure and male sterility due to cyclophosphamide, are important considerations. Because the efficacy of immunosuppressive therapy in certain diseases is often difficult to establish, physicians must bear in mind the risks entailed before starting treatment. Such proof will only be obtained after meticulously executed control therapeutic trials. A beginning has already been made, and Table 24 lists some of the results.

Table 24
Controlled clinical trials of immunosuppressive therapy

Disease	Drug	Result
Rheumatoid arthritis	Azathioprine	Effective
Rheumatoid arthritis	Cyclophosphamide	Effective
Psoriatic arthritis	Methotrexate	Effective
Psoriatic arthritis	Azathioprine	Effective
SLE	Azathioprine	Effective
Regional enteritis	Azathioprine	Ineffective
Chronic active hepatitis	Azathioprine	Probably effective
Chronic active hepatitis	Chlorambucil	Ineffective
Childhood nephrotic syndrome	Cyclophosphamide	Effective
Childhood nephrotic syndrome	Azathioprine	Ineffective
Adult nephrotic syndrome	Azathioprine	Ineffective
Chronic glomerulonephritis	Azathioprine	Ineffective
Multiple sclerosis	Cyclophosphamide	Ineffective
Bronchial asthma	6-mercaptopurine	Ineffective

Future Prospects

The extraordinary advances in immunology and molecular biology that have occurred during the past ten years will surely have an equally extraordinary impact on clinical medicine during the next decade. As the fascinating details of the immunologic network are unraveled, we become increasingly aware of their significance in the solution of many immunologic diseases, including allergic and autoimmune disorders. For example, certain allergic diseases may reflect the genetic inability of specific subsets of suppressor cells to regulate the synthesis of IgE. There is increasing evidence that some autoimmune diseases are due not only to intrinsically impaired immunoregulation but also to "outlaw" B cells that fail to obey normal regulatory signals.

Perhaps the most meaningful immunologic principle that has emerged in the past ten years is that lymphocytes and macrophages communicate with each other by means of signals that are perceived at the cell surface. The immunologic code – the signals – will ultimately be deciphered, at which time an entirely new level of understanding will have been achieved. In the meantime, we already know that highly specific antibodies against some of the signals (receptors, cell surface structures) can be prepared. By combining the technologies of immunology, molecular biology, and somatic cell hybridization, it is or will be possible, in principle, to manufacture in vitro

□ human antibodies of any desired specificity
□ lymphocyte mediators (eg, helper or suppressor signals) of any specificity
□ artificial membranes that contain only those structures desired for clinical purposes (eg, immunogenic tumor-specific antigens embedded within an artificial lipid bilayer)
□ human antibodies that will stimulate cells (eg, antibodies that can react with receptors for insulin and thereby replace the need for the hormone)
□ synthetic compounds that will react with specific receptors on the surfaces of lymphoid cells (eg, "drugs" that act as ligands and block or stimulate specific subsets of lymphocytes)

Futuristic as these prospects may seem, the technology required to achieve these goals is now in an advanced stage of development. There is every reason to believe that such new forms of immunologic manipulation will come to fruition.

Acknowledgments

Figure 1
Reproduced with permission from the Journal of Experimental Medicine (118:327, 1963).

Figures 5a, 5b
With permission from Journal of Molecular Biology (27:615, 1967). Copyright by Academic Press Inc. (London) Ltd.

Figure 7
Reproduced with permission of C. E. Miller, MD, Beckman Instruments, Fullerton, CA.

Figures 8, 9, 10
Adapted, with permission, from Eisen HN: *Immunology,* Harper & Row, Hagerstown, MD, © 1974.

Figure 11
Reproduced with permission of M. A. MacDonald, MD, Kalamazoo, MI.

Figure 12
Reproduced with permission of H. G. Johnson, PhD, The Upjohn Company, Kalamazoo, MI.

Figures 16, 17
Reproduced with permission of B. Unavas, MD, Karolinska Institute, Stockholm.

Figure 18
Reproduced with permission of J. L. Mongar, MD, University College, London.

Figures 19, 20
Reproduced with permission of A. B. Kay, MD, Cardiothoracic Institute, University of London, London.

Figure 22
Adapted with permission of K. F. Austen, MD, Harvard Medical School, Boston, MA.

Figure 26
Reproduced with permission of The American Journal of Pathology (53:243, 1968).

Figure 27
Reproduced with permission of R. Dourmashkin, MD, National Institute for Medical Research, London.

Figure 42
Reproduced with permission of E. M. Block, PhD, The Upjohn Company, Kalamazoo, MI.

Figures 49, 50
Reproduced with permission of J. L. Turk, MD, Royal College of Surgeons of England, London.

Figures 45, 46
From the Department of Dermatology, London Hospital Medical College, London.

Figure 52
Reproduced with permission of Journal of Immunology (93:264, 1964). © 1964 The Williams & Wilkins Co., Baltimore.

Figure 54
Reproduced with permission of T. H. Flewett, MD, Regional Virus Laboratory, Birmingham, England.

Figures 61, 63
Reproduced with permission of MEDCOM, New York.

Figure 62
Reproduced with permission of L. T. Old, MD, Memorial Sloan-Kettering Cancer Center, New York.

Figure 70
Reproduced with permission of George Santos, MD, The Johns Hopkins University School of Medicine, Baltimore.

Figure 71
Reproduced with permission of the Medical Department, The British Council.

Figure 72
Adapted with permission: Dausset J, Svejgaard A: *HLA and Disease.* Copenhagen, Munksgaard and Baltimore, The Williams & Wilkins Co., © 1977.

Figure 73
Adapted with permission of *Tissue Antigens* (11:113-120, 1978).

Figure 74
Adapted with permission of the New England Journal of Medicine (299:911-915, 1978).

Figure 81
Reproduced with permission of Cancer Research (27:2578-2615, 1967).

Table 22
Reproduced with permission, Ryder LP, Anderson E, Svejgaard A: *HLA and Disease Registry, Third Report.* Munksgaard, Copenhagen, 1979.

Index